CZECHOSLOVAKIAN

GLASS & COLLECTIBLES

❖ BOOK II ❖

IDENTIFICATION & VALUE GUIDE

Dale and Diane Barta

Helen M. Rose

COLLECTOR BOOKS

A Division of Schroeder Publishing Co., Inc.

The current values in this book should be used only as a guide. They are not intended to set prices, which vary from one section of the country to another. Auction prices as well as dealer prices vary greatly and are affected by condition as well as demand. Neither the Authors nor the Publisher assumes responsibility for any losses that might be incurred as a result of consulting this guide.

Searching For A Publisher?

We are always looking for knowledgeable people considered to be experts within their fields. If you feel that there is a real need for a book on your collectible subject and have a large comprehensive collection, contact Collector Books.

Front cover:

Vase, 14½", Amphora, Egyptian motif, King Tut, tile inlay, light blue, dark blue, and white, body beige stipple effect, $400.00 – 450.00.

Vase, 8¼", orange with blue, cased, satin glass, $60.00 – 70.00.

Glass atomizer base, 6¼", clear glass with hand-painted enamel scene, Middle Eastern desert oasis with palm trees with camel and man done in black silhouette, silver tone metal top, $145.00 – 150.00.

Pin, 2", silver tone spider setting with red glass large center stone, $20.00 – 25.00.

Dresser box, 4½", porcelain, 6-sided, pale center design of blue-green, blue, and light green on raised design of flower garland, dark orange and yellow base and lid, allover basket weave design, braided band at top and bottom of the base, knob on the lid is a rose, $45.00 – 50.00.

Planter, 11", lady figurine, white, Art Deco look, $135.00 – 140.00.

Back cover:

Ewer, 9½", high green relief, Chris 1492 on front, Isabel 1492, on back, $85.00 – 90.00.

Cover design by Beth Summers
Book design by Beth Ray

Additional copies of this book may be ordered from:

COLLECTOR BOOKS
P.O. Box 3009
Paducah, Kentucky 42002-3009

@$16.95. Add $2.00 for postage and handling.

Copyright: Dale and Diane Barta, Helen M. Rose, 1997

CONTENTS

DEDICATION

We dedicate this book to all the old friends and collectors we know, and to all the new friends and collectors we have yet to meet. May your collecting give you lots of happy hours and your lifetime lots of happy memories.

 # INTRODUCTION

To all the Czechoslovakian collectors and dealers "hello," we are back again, with Book II. We must thank all of you who supported our efforts with Book I.

Some things have changed since we wrote the first book. Most collectible items of Czechoslovakian origin have fallen into the time span of 1918 through 1938, a twenty-year span when glass and pottery production was at its highest.

In January of 1993 Czechoslovakia broke into two separate republics. We now have the Czech Republic and the Slovak Republic; all items will reflect this division. This means items marked Czech-Slovakia or Czechoslovakia are now all collectibles. Newer items will be less expensive to buy, and less coveted. This will probably be a starting point for new collectors or even those of us on a budget. We know that nothing stays the same; all things change, some for the good and some for the bad. We hope the people of both republics will find peace and contentment in their lives. After their tragic past, they all deserve happiness.

This book is divided into ten sections. Examples in all categories are different than those shown in Book I.

In Section I, Pottery, Porcelain, and China, there is a great variety of types from expensive down to inexpensive. How pieces that can be from 60 to 80 years old have survived is a miracle in itself. Most pieces in this section are common pottery, Erphila, Peasant Art, and the very high end of Amphora. There still is a vast array of different items yet to be found. You have to keep on searching the market places.

The second section is Glass. There is a lot of variety in styles and types. Most glass pieces speak for themselves. It doesn't matter if the piece is single or cased glass, with decoration or without, each is indeed beautiful and unusual. Examples of both glass and crystal are shown.

The third section is Barrels and Eggs. This will be found at the end of the glass section. The barrels hold liquid of one kind or another. The eggs hold beverage sets consisting of a decanter and glasses. These beverage sets in different shapes are rather unique. In California, in the good old days, they were given away as carnival prizes. I don't know if other states did the same. Most of the metal on these sets is either nickel or nickel plated. Most of the photos are from a fellow collector, Mary Gunderson. We also thank her for the copy of the page from the Butler Bros. catalog, showing pieces as they originally looked.

Section four is Perfumes and Colognes. This is where the Czechs really shone. All of the different and unusual bases in crystal and drop stoppers cannot be compared to any others. The quality and the workmanship outshine all the others. You can find plain and simple to very elaborate bases, bottles, and stoppers. But the beauty of a simple design cannot and should not be overlooked. We think the array of items in this section shows a lot of variety.

Section five is on Moser and Bohemian Glass. It is a small section, again just to show the older pieces and the artistry. Even though they have their own categories, they are the older and higher quality Czechoslovakian pieces.

Section six is Jewelry and Buckles. This jewelry section shows a lot more examples this time. We found several different pieces in many different price ranges. What follows is a bit of history on Czech glass beads.

Starting in the eighth century as rosary makers for a local monastery, the glassmakers later developed glass versions of cut garnet stones. By 1750, Bohemia was a major exporter of trade beads to the world. Her sample men (salesmen) traveled around the world to collect native jewelry to be reproduced in glass. Shells, hippo teeth, cowries, bone beads, interlocking "snake" beads, "ancient" beads from Korea, Japan, India, and Tibet were marketed from the glasshouses of Bohemia.

Garnet jewelry (from garnets mined in the Turnor area of Bohemia), beautiful costume jewelry, and beautiful cut glass were known the world over. It is not generally known that Czechs are renowned for making fine, colorful, highly lustrous glass beads. European traders in the fourteenth century actually traded these beads with the North American Indians for furs, hides, and horses.

The glass beads were introduced to America by Christopher Columbus when he presented a necklace of red beads to the natives of San Salvador in 1492. Francisco Vasques de Coronado, the Spanish explorer, brought glass beads that he exchanged for food and lodging in 1541 to the plains of Kansas. During the same time frame, other explorers took identical beads to Asia and Africa. Like the Indians of the Americas, these inhabitants were just as pleased with the beads.

A cobalt blue, many faceted bead made in Bohemia expressly for Russian exploration was called the "Russian blue." The natives of Alaska were introduced to this bead by Vitus Bering, an explorer. This was to become the most sought-after bead by the Northwest Indians. They called it the "chief" bead. It was called the "ambassador" in Africa where it was also popular.

Between 1915 and 1920 the last bead called the "Hubbell" was made. It came in many shapes and sizes and shades of the same color. It was requested by Lorenzo Hubbell to trade with North American Indians. It was designed to imitate turquoise. Lorenzo wanted it for his Hubbell Trading Post in Gavado, Arizona.

The Czech glass beads are still the most desirable beadwork even today.

From the beginnings of glass bead-making learned on the island of Murano, Italy, through two world wars and the turmoil of communist control of the area, the Czech bead industry was rearranged but not destroyed. Adaptable and creative, the glasshouses have sent their experts to establish glass bead industries in other European cities, and in India and China. We hope the beads keep on coming.

The seventh section is Purses. What can we say — more unique and beautiful designs. More patterns using Czech glass beads and pearls. They are definitely eye catching and lovely.

The eighth section is Lamps. This is another small section. The styles are all a little different. The array shows a good range of materials used. There are faceted glass beads, fruit, and metal with intaglio cut crystal discs. There is also a vanity perfume lamp and a tall candlestick base lamp with a chimney and a globe.

Section nine is New Glass and Collectibles. This section deals with newer items that were still made in Czechoslovakia, but have some of the newer stickers on them, including crystal vases and decanter sets and little crystal knick-knacks. These are still in the collectible category, only a little newer.

The tenth section covers Uncommon Items, Toys, and Miscellaneous. This takes in all other items that do not have a category, such as guns, place card holders, linens, and Christmas ornaments. We also have beaded items and picture frames. Toys are always interesting and we show examples of them, also.

We really hope you enjoy the book. We enjoyed collecting and putting this book together. We hope you have good luck in your search for Czech items.

Please remember all measurements are approximate; most of the measurements are for height.

VALUE GUIDE

The values here reflect what is currently being quoted and asked by dealers or collectors. The values for the pieces in this book are merely here as a guide. We have tried to give a range in which the item will fall. The price will depend on where you live.

We have visited quite a few antique shops and several auctions. We have talked to dealers and collectors from several states, which has helped in establishing the prices.

Czechoslovakian items are still gaining in popularity and are still attracting new collectors. As this continues to happen, the pieces keep disappearing and the prices keep rising. You may find that some pieces are either higher or lower than the range you find here. As with all things, it is what the market will bear and the availability of some items in your area that will ultimately set the prices.

The values in the guide are for pieces in mint condition. Remember the rarity of an item will bring into play the prices set by the dealer. Remember to check the items carefully; any damage will affect the asking price. Remember the best advice is still: BUYER BEWARE!

POTTERY, PORCELAIN, AND CHINA

(1) Lady toothbrush holder, 8", Erphila, white and blue dress, $30.00 – 40.00. (2) Figurine, 9½", girl with grapes, black and white, glazed, $90.00 – 100.00. (3) Vase, 5", angel with horn of plenty, $20.00 – 25.00.

Vase, 11", Amphora, beige with boy and girl, $750.00 – 800.00.

Vase, 11¼", Amphora, Egyptian motif, $400.00 – 450.00.

Pitcher, 10", 6 tumblers, 4", cream with red and purple grapes. Pitcher has purple handle, $170.00 – 175.00 set.

(1) Vase, 4½", blue, pink flowers, green leaves, $30.00 – 35.00. (2) Vase 3¾", blue, scene girls pulling cupid in wagon, $25.00 – 30.00. (3) Pitcher, 3", white with green designs, $15.00 – 20.00.

(1) Pitcher, 7½", Amphora, blue with flower medallion, hi-gloss blue handle, $80.00 – 85.00. (2) Ewer, 9½", Erphila, green sea serpent handles, beige, green rim and base, high relief face and birds, $125.00 – 135.00.

(1) Ewer, 9½", high relief green, Chris 1492 on front, Isabel 1492 on back. $85.00 – 90.00.

From the collection of Mary Gunderson

Boat, 10¼", white outside, green glaze on the inside, could be for trinkets or for candy, $30.00 – 40.00.

From the collection of Mary Gunderson

(1) Tom and Jerry cup, 3", words written in gold, also gold bands encircle the cup, $20.00 – 25.00. (2) Cup, 3½" high x 3" across, pale orange or tan lusterware, red rim, blue and red alternating bands encircle the cup, $25.00 – 30.00. (3) Handle, 4" long, white background with green and pink design, heavy pottery, $20.00 – 25.00.

Pair funeral vases, 11¾", yellow and blue with white and green enameling, $75.00 – 80.00 a pair.

(1) Planter, 5", yellow with black and white design, $25.00 – 30.00. (2) Candlestick holder, 2¼", yellow with black and white design, $35.00 – 40.00. (3) Vase, 6½", yellow with black and white design, $30.00 – 35.00.

(1) Vase, 5¼", orange and white with black rim, $30.00 – 35.00. (2) Vase, 5", burnt orange with enameled blue flowers, $35.00 – 45.00. (3) Toby mug, 5¼", Bumble, $50.00 – 55.00.

(1) Covered pancake batter pitcher, Erphila, white and green, orange trim and poppies, $50.00 – 55.00. (2) Covered syrup, 5¼", Erphila, white and green, orange trim and poppies, $45.00 – 50.00.

Row A: (1) Pitcher, 7", light green with dark green spout, monastery scene, $50.00 – 55.00. (2) Pitcher, 7½", Bohemian, beige, blue, pink, yellow, brown handle, $45.00 – 50.00.
Row B: (1) Vase, 8¾", blue with white and black trim, flowers, $35.00 – 40.00. (2) Bowl, 3", peasant art, black with orange flower, $20.00 – 25.00. (3) Bud vase, 7", orange flowers, bluebird marking, $50.00 – 55.00.

Row A: (1) Pedestal candleholder, 4¼", Egyptian motif, green with blue head and green face, $50.00 – 55.00. (2) Cigarette holder, 3", brown, $10.00 – 12.00. (3) Bowl, 4", green with elephant, $30.00 – 40.00.
Row B: (1) Candleholders, 6", pair, green mottled luster, $40.00 – 45.00. (2) Cut flower holder, 7¼", orange with flowers, black frog top and black base, $55.00 – 60.00.

Planter, 11", lady figurine, white, art deco look, $135.00 – 140.00.

Baby dish, 1½" deep x 7" across, green mottled sides and band on the bottom, children's scene in the center, "baby" is written in silver script, $40.00 – 45.00.

Platter bowl, 9", hand painted, teal, orange, gray, and white design, rolled handles, high gloss finish, $40.00 – 45.00.

(1) Figurine, 4", dog, black and white, $30.00 – 35.00. (2) Figurine, 5", cat, white and pink, $40.00 – 45.00. (3) Toothpick holder, 2", Erphila, rooster, cream and red, $25.00 – 30.00.

Vase, 10½", white with Oriental scene, red and gold flecked handles. Marked Czecho-Slovakia and Chinese marking, $250.00 – 255.00.

(1) Mustard pot, 3½", white with pansy and black trim, $45.00 – 50.00 (2) Vase, 7", white, flowers, black rim and base, $50.00 – 55.00.

(1) Vase, 11½", yellow with purple, red and green flowers, black swirls, blue top and base, $75.00 – 80.00. (2) Vase, 11", yellow with purple, red and green flowers, black swirls, blue top and base, $75.00 – 80.00.

(1) Pitcher, 7½", chicken, white, red and black $50.00 – 55.00. (2) Pitcher, 9", Erphila, toucan, cream, red and black, $85.00 – 90.00.

(1) Planter, 4¼", Erphila, beige with black silhouette woman and children, $50.00 – 55.00. (2) Vase, 7", Erphila, beige with black silhouette girl with goat, $60.00 – 65.00.

(1) Ewer, 11½", purple, black, red, matte finish, $60.00 – 65.00. (2) Ewer, 8", purple, red, black, black matte base and top, $55.00 – 60.00.

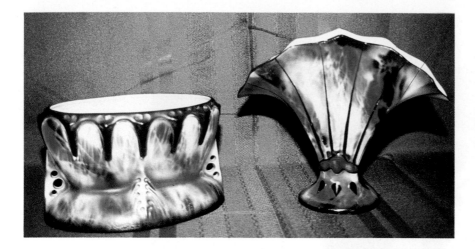

(1) Planter, 4½", purple, red, black, matte finish, $50.00 – 55.00. (2) Fan vase, 7½", mauve, orange, black with blue design, $65.00 – 70.00.

(1) Vase, 7¾", white with green cactus, orange flower, pink flowers, trimmed in blue, $40.00 – 45.00. (2) Ewer, 7", beige, farm scene, green base and deco, $55.00 – 60.00.

Pitcher, 7¼", Erphila, blue and white, colored bubbles, air brushed, $65.00 – 70.00.

Demitasse cups, 2¾", 3 white cups, one yellow trim, one blue trim and one green trim, $7.50 each.

Demitasse cups, 2¾", 4 white cups, one dark green trim, one black trim, one light blue trim and one red trim, $7.50 each.

(1) Basket pottery, 4¾", design of air brushed circles with geometric lines, done in shades of blue and orange with white, $40.00 – 45.00. (2) Pitcher, 4¾", pottery, design of air brushed circles with geometric lines, done in shades of blue and orange with white, $50.00 – 55.00.

Wall pocket, 5", pottery, green limb with a birdhouse in brownish orange, with small bird done in multi colors, $60.00 – 65.00.

Milk pitcher, 6", yellow shaded base, and handle, dark blue rim and detail on the handle, turquoise shading from the top down to the middle, design of multicolored flowers in the center, $70.00 – 75.00.

(1) Creamer, 2½", white with design of center medallion with a mythical creature on either side, handle and rim done in orange, $20.00 – 25.00. (2) Creamer, 3½", red panels with white panels, stipple design on the white, red handle with white interior, $20.00 – 25.00.

Vase, 8", blue mottled pearlescent color, $45.00 – 50.00.

Vase, 10", yellow lusterware, fluted black rim, double handles, $45.00 – 50.00.

Vase, 5¼", vanity set possibly, bright orange with garland of flowers around the vase, flowers are yellow with green leaves, detailing done in black, $35.00 – 40.00.

From the collection of Mary Gunderson

(1) Spice canister, 4", cinnamon, white with a black design of a man and woman in silhouette, with the rest of the design in black, $15.00 – 20.00. (2) Spice canister, 4", cloves, white with a black design of a man and woman in silhouette, with the rest of the design in black, $15.00 – 20.00. (3) Cruet, 9", oil, white with a black design of a man and woman in silhouette, with the rest of the design in black, $35.00 – 40.00. (4) Spice canister, 4", nutmeg, white with a black design of a man and woman in silhouette, with the rest of the design in black, $15.00 – 20.00. (5) Spice canister, 4", ginger, white with a black design of a man and woman in silhouette, with the rest of the design in black, $15.00 – 20.00. (6) Spice canister, 4", allspice, white with a black design of a man and woman in silhouette, with the rest of the design in black, $15.00 – 20.00.

Canister, 8¼", off-white with scenic view of a tree-lined river with colorful flowers in the foreground, $40.00 – 45.00.

From the collection of Mary Gunderson

(1) Pitcher, 6¼", teal blue with black, white, orange and green design, made like a feathered Indian design, $45.00 – 50.00. (2) Creamer, 3½", peasant art pottery, yellow interior, with flower design of orange, yellow, blue, burgundy and green, black rim and handle, $50.00 – 55.00. (3) Pitcher, 5½", gray and white mottled background with hand-painted design of fruit and leaves, $35.00 – 40.00.

(1) Covered vase, 7", brown and white with gold trim, Roman scene with man, woman and cherub, $60.00 – 65.00. (2) Vase, 8¼", green and yellow design with black top, handles and base, $50.00 – 55.00. (3) Vase, 5", white with yellow, orange, black, and green flower design, black rim, $40.00 – 45.00.

(1) Pitcher, 5¼", tri-corner spouts, burgundy and white with black mottling, black handle and rim, $45.00 – 50.00. (2) Basket, 5", heart cut-out handle, light green background with multicolored carnations, $30.00 – 40.00.

Vase, 4¾", very bright variegated pastel colors with high gloss finish. Two variations of glaze shown. $45.00 – 50.00 each.

(1) Planter, 3¼" tall x 4" across, with pedestal base, blue-green with orange, blue, yellow, green, and red design, $50.00 – 55.00. (2) Lady figurine, 5¼", with small plant holder, pastel coloring with red and black trim, $55.00 – 60.00.

Planter bowl, 6½" across, white pearlescent with bluebird on the side, two applied birds on rim, $50.00 – 55.00.

(1) Bird flower holder, 6", brown and green base with rust, blue and brown parrot, $35.00 – 40.00. (2) Bell, 4¼", pearlescent center with orange top and rim, black detail, $30.00 – 35.00. (3) Bird flower holder, 4½", green base with blue, yellow, brown, and orange small bird, $35.00 – 40.00.

Flower holder, 9", brown tree base with orange, green, and yellow woodpecker, $45.00 – 50.00.

Pitcher, 7½", bright yellow with blue rim and handle, $40.00 – 45.00.

Vase, 11", yellow orange lusterware with black trim, $40.00 – 45.00.

(1) Vase, 4¼", white pottery bowl with applied glass flower and leaves, $35.00 – 40.00. (2) Sugar bowl, 2¼", white grape design, open top, $25.00 – 30.00. (3) Creamer, 4", white grape and leaf design, vine handle, $25.00 – 30.00.

(1) Child's set, 1¼", sugar bowl, open style, white background with pink rim and pink band around the base, center design of pink flowers and leaves, Erphila, $25.00 – 30.00. (2) Child's set, 2¾", creamer, white background with rust color rim and detail on the fancy handle, pink band on base, center design in pink of flowers and leaves, Erphila, $25.00 – 30.00.

(1) Ashtray, 5", bright white seashell design, Erphila, $35.00 – 40.00. (2) Crab, 4½", either a melted butter dish with lid, or a trinket box with lid for the vanity, red with black accents, $25.00 – 30.00.

(1) Creamer, 3¼" round design in bright canary yellow, interior is white, $20.00 – 25.00. (2) Milk pitcher, 4½", bright red body with white handle and white interior, (no price listed for this item).

Covered box, 3" x 6", yellow with a large red flower with green leaves, red bud with leaves on lid, for trinkets, $40.00 – 45.00.

Covered box, 2¼" x 5¼", white interior, orange luster on outside, black and gray fish on lid, man's trinket box, $40.00 – 45.00.

Covered box, 4¼", duck shape, painted with several muted colors, man's trinket box, or covered sugar when together with duck creamer, $40.00 – 45.00.

(1) Figurine, 5½", white horse, pottery, $45.00 – 50.00. (2) Basket planter, 8¼", white with pressed design, $40.00 – 45.00. (3) Figurine, 4½", white horse, pottery, $40.00 – 45.00.

(1) Figurine, 7½", stork planter, black and pearlescent, pottery, $60.00 – 65.00. (2) Vase, 6½", pink, green, yellow, and blue pastels with gold and black top design, $50.00 – 55.00. (3) Figurine, 6" stork planter, pastel colors with green and brown base, pottery, $50.00 – 55.00.

Figurine, 3¾", dog, white with light and dark green spots on body, shaded on nose and ears, pink collar and tongue, black accents, raised paw with bug on it. Bug is made of metal, $60.00 – 65.00.

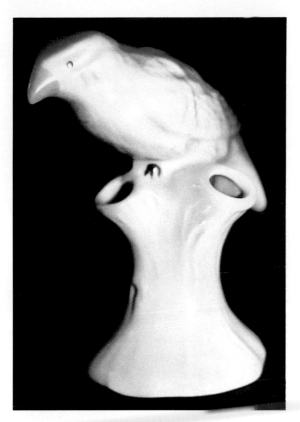

Flower holder, 4½", bird, green tree stump, with 3 holes, small multicolored bird on top, $40.00 – 45.00.

(1) Flower holder, 5½", bird, yellow double branch base, 2 holes, has bird on top in shades of rust, yellow, and blue, $45.00 – 50.00. (2) Camel, 2", cigarettes and match holder, camel in shades of orange with beige cigarette and match holder done in the design of a travel box with 6 round carriers, (no price listed for this item).

(1) Plate, 7¾", 8-sided; (2) Plate, 5½", saucer, 6-sided; (3) Cup, 2" x 3¾" across, 6-sided; (4) Sugar bowl and lid, 4½", 6-sided; (5) Creamer, 2½", 6-sided; (6) Teapot with lid, 6", 6-sided. 23-piece tea set, all pieces are purple iridescent with white, opalescent in center of plates and interior of cup, gold borders and rims, handles, finials, and other detailing. Sold as a set, $150.00 – 200.00.

(1) Toby mug, 1¾", pottery, woman, painted in colors of brown, blue, green with black detail, $40.00 – 45.00. (2) Pitcher, 3", toothpick holder, white with a flower design and blue rim, $40.00 – 45.00. (3) Candle holder, 3", metal base, goldtone with design and faceted green glass stones, top is satin glass, multi-shades of green, $30.00 – 35.00. (4) Pitcher, 1½", miniature, green outside with white interior, double stamped Czechoslovakia and Germany, $40.00 – 45.00.

(1) Vase, 4¾", with 2 small ear handles, mottled colors of blue, green, orange, yellow, and white in a design, with purple interior, high gloss, $40.00 – 45.00. (2) Vase, 8", mottled colors of blue, green, orange, yellow, and white in a design, purple interior, high gloss, $55.00 – 60.00. (3) Same as (1), $40.00 – 45.00.

(1) Chicken figurine, 6¾", white with orange, green, gold, red, and black detail, Erphila, $55.00 – 60.00. (2) Rooster figurine, 7⅛", white with green, orange, gold, red, and black detail, Erphila, $55.00 – 60.00.

(1) Candlestick holder, 1½" high x 4½" wide, tan luster inside, painted Oriental scene around outside, black handle and rim, $45.00 – 50.00. (2) Planter bowl, 2¾" high x 5½" wide, white interior with painted Oriental scene around outside, black handles and rim, $40.00 – 45.00.

Match holder, 5", green interior with hand painted Oriental scene, also gold fish scene, hard to find, $65.00 – 70.00.

(1) Mug, 4¼", heavyweight, white with center scene in a medallion, tavern scene of man drinking with woman playing mandolin, cat at her feet. Erphila pottery, $30.00 – 35.00. (2) Mug, 4¼", heavyweight, white with center scene in a medallion, tavern scene of 1 man drinking with 1 woman and singing, 1 man playing a mandolin, Erphila pottery, $30.00 – 35.00.

(1) Mug, 4¼", heavyweight, white with center scene in a medallion, tavern scene of 2 European men in Bavarian costume being served by Bavarian woman, a small dachshund in the foreground, Erphila pottery, $30.00 – 35.00. (2) Mug, 4¼", heavyweight, white with center scene in a medallion, tavern scene of 2 friars or brothers drinking ale with a European man in Bavarian costume, Erphila pottery, $30.00 – 35.00.

(1) Pitcher, 8⅛", cream color background, with raised relief design of painted fruits with leaves, assorted fruits and colors, yellow, pink, and blue bands around top, blue handle. (2) Glasses, 4" tall, set of 6, cream color background, with raised relief design of painted fruits with leaves, assorted fruits and colors, yellow and blue bands around the top, also a brown vine around each glass. Sold as a set, $150.00 – 155.00.

(1) Pitcher, 7¾", white background with red and green bands alternately around the pitcher in between the ridges, white handle with red trim and red rim, $40.00 – 45.00.
(2) Pitcher, 7½", flared-out top, yellow background with decorative orange handle, orange band all around the base and around the rim, freestyle hand-painted design, colors of orange, green, blue, and black, $50.00 – 55.00.

(1) Nut bowl, 5½" across, flower shape in colors of blue, white, and orange, $15.00 – 20.00.
(2) Nut bowl, 6" across, flower shape in colors of blue, white, orange, and green, high gloss, $15.00 – 20.00.

(1) Nut bowl, 6" across, flower shape in colors of blue, yellow, orange, and green, high gloss, $15.00 – 20.00. (2) Nut bowl, 6½" across, flower shape in colors of blue, white, yellow, orange, and green, high gloss, $15.00 – 20.00.

From the collection of Alfred W. Giordano

Nut bowl, 6" across, flower shape in colors of blue, green, white, and orange, high gloss, $15.00 – 20.00.

(1) Plate, Tartan plaid, with brown, light green, tan, red, and black. matches mugs in Book 1, Erphila, $25.00 – 30.00. (2) Pot, coffee or tea server, approximately 8" tall, Tartan plaid, with brown, light green, tan, red, and black. Matches Tartan mugs in Book 1, Erphila, $50.00 – 55.00.

(1) Saucer, 3½" across, with 1¾" tall cup, yellow with white under saucer and in the interior of the cup, black handle with black rim on the cup and saucer, child's set, $15.00 – 20.00. (2) Sugar bowl, 1¾", missing lid, yellow with white interior, black rim, 2 black handles, child's set, $15.00 – 20.00. (3) Saucer, 3½" across, with 1¾" tall cup, yellow with white under saucer and in the interior of the cup, black handle with black rim on the cup and saucer, same as (1) child's set, $15.00 – 20.00.

Candy dish, 6" across, floral, cut-out on sides, $40.00 – 45.00.

Erphila floral ashtray, 3¾", $25.00 – 30.00.

Erphila large yellow bowl, 10¾", $15.00 – 20.00.

Creamer, 2¼", silver and white, $15.00 – 20.00.

Pitcher, 7½", orange with black handle and rim, $20.00 – 25.00.

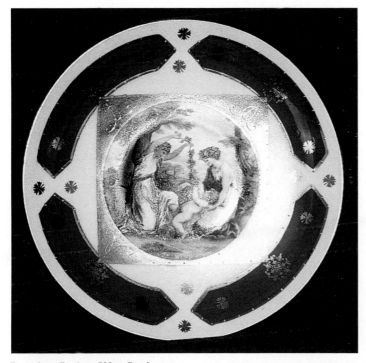

From the collection of Mary Gunderson

Plate, 6" across, embossed, hand painted and decaled, has artist's signature on front in burgundy letters: "Angelica Kauffman," very nice decorator's plate, $60.00 – 65.00.

Plate, 11", has outer border design and inner border design, center has the picture of a woman, with brown background, hand painted, another example of a beautiful decorator's plate, $60.00 – 65.00.

From the collection of Mary Gunderson

From the collection of Mary Gunderson

Leaf design plate, 6" across x 7" long, with a nut-shaped bowl attached in the center, off-white color, lid is missing, $40.00 – 45.00.

From the collection of Mary Gunderson

Two-handled dish, 7" long x 4¼" wide, all gold overlay with embossed flower basket design, $45.00 – 50.00.

(1) Creamer, 3¾", pearlescent lusterware, green rim and green handle, $20.00 – 25.00. (2) Creamer, 2½", white with bands of pale green lusterware, $20.00 – 25.00. (3) Creamer, 3½", shaded yellow top, white background on base, with raised relief design, orange diamonds with blue outlining, white handle, top has black rim, $30.00 – 35.00.

(1) Creamer, 2½", yellow pearlescent, with black handle and black rim, $20.00 – 25.00. (2) Open sugar, 2", petal design bowl, pale yellow opalescent with black rim, $20.00 – 25.00. (3) Creamer, 3", pedestal base, light orange lusterware, black handle with black rim, $20.00 – 25.00.

(1) Creamer, 3½", pale orange or tan lusterware, black handle with black rim, $20.00 – 25.00. (2) Vase, 5½", pale yellow lusterware, black handles, with black rim, $20.00 – 25.00. (3) Creamer, 3¾", pale yellow lusterware, with black handle and black rim, $20.00 – 25.00.

(1) Creamer, 3¾", wood grain, cedar, multi-shades of brown, dark brown band around the creamer, white handle with a black rim, white interior, $25.00 – 30.00. (2) Creamer, 3½", wood grain, with wood grain handle, multi-shades of brown, black bands around the center, top and bottom, white interior, $25.00 – 30.00.

Milk pitcher, 5¾", wood grain, cedar, multi-shades of brown, dark brown line around the pitcher, white handle, black band around the rim, $40.00 – 45.00.

(1) Watering can, 5¼", white background with blue-green shading and trim, center design of 2 swans in the water, $45.00 – 50.00. (2) Basket, 5¼", beige with orange shading and orange handle, blue band around rim, $40.00 – 45.00.

(1) Creamer, 3", moose lying down, open mouth, white pearl opalescent, full antlers, blue handle, black eyes, unusual, $50.00 – 55.00. (2) Creamer, 3½", water buffalo, open mouth, shades of beige, brown, and light green, beige and brown handle, black trim on nose, eyes, and ears, high relief picture of person milking a cow in the center on both sides, full horns, very rare, $60.00 – 65.00.

(1) Milk pitcher, 3¾", white with pearlescent design and handle, red trim on handle and on rim, a set of 4 raised bumps on 3 sides colored in red, green, blue, and yellow, $40.00 – 45.00. (2) Milk pitcher, 4¾", white background with green detail and trim on handle, center design of man and woman holding a large heart, design done in red and green with white, dressed in European costumes, $40.00 – 45.00.

(1) Creamer, 3", white with black rim and black trim on handle, design of rust, green and yellow, all detail done in black, $35.00 – 40.00. (2) Creamer, 3¼", white with red trim on the handle, center design of man and woman holding a large heart, done in colors of red, black, and white, European costumes, $35.00 – 40.00.

(1) Creamer, 3¼", pink lusterware top, also handle, green lusterware bottom, black band around the center with black rim, white interior, $35.00 – 40.00. (2) Creamer, 4¼", light and dark mixed orange background, hand painted flower medallion in the center, colors of blue, red, yellow, pink, and green, black detail with black handle and rim, $35.00 – 40.00.

(1) Creamer, 4", moose, open mouth, beige with shades of brown, light blue base, black trim on mouth and eyes, full set of antlers, beige and brown shaded handle, $45.00 – 50.00. (2) Creamer, 3¾", water buffalo, open mouth, beige with shades of brown, light blue base, trim on eyes done in black, full horns, beige and brown shaded handle, rarely seen, $45.00 – 50.00.

(1) Creamer, 3¼" tall x 6¼" long, cow lying down, open mouth, colors of beige with shades of brown handle, mouth and horns are lighter, $45.00 – 50.00. (2) Creamer, 4", Toby mug, man, base, rim and the handle are done in lavender, man with white hair, blue coat with yellow and green pants, green vest, black shoes, holding green mug, red and black trim, $45.00 – 50.00.

(1) Honey pot with saucer, 6¼", pale green with red flowers and green leaves, $40.00 – 45.00. (2) Jam pot with saucer, 3½", pale blue with pink, white, and darker blue, $40.00 – 45.00.

(1) Sugar, 2", creamer, 3¼", orange, white, Niagara Falls, $35.00 – 40.00 a set. (2) Creamer, 3", white with dancers, red and green, $15.00 – 20.00.

(1) Juicer, 4", mustard with black handle and rim, white interior, $20.00 – 25.00. (2) Yellow plant saucer, 6¾", black and white design, $15.00 – 20.00.

(1) Planter, 2¾", Erphila, desert scene brown, beige, reddish brown, and brown handles, $40.00 – 45.00. (2) Pitcher, 4", leaves, rust, blue, and yellow, $25.00 – 30.00.

(1) Creamer, 2½", mauve with darker handle, $15.00 – 20.00. (2) Creamer, 4½", pearl lusterware with blue handle and rim, $25.00 – 30.00. (3) Creamer, 2", orange lusterware with green inside, $20.00 – 25.00.

(1) Basket, candy or nut, 4¼", lusterware, applied orange handle, $20.00 – 25.00. (2) Creamer, 3", lusterware, applied orange handle, $15.00 – 20.00.

Vase, 6½", white with flowers, applied orange handles, orange rim and base, $35.00 – 40.00.

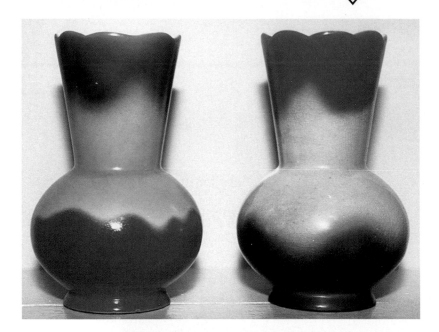

(1) Vase, 5", blue, yellow, and red, $20.00 – 25.00. (2) Vase, 5", red, cream, and blue, $20.00 – 25.00.

(1) Saucer, 4½" across, cup, 1½" tall x 3" across; (2) Teapot with lid; 6½"; (3) Sugar bowl with lid, 3"; (4) Creamer, 3½". 21-piece child's tea set, purple, red, and gray design with gold detail, high gloss finish, $90.00 – 95.00 set.

(1) Swan design sugar bowl and lid, 2½", colors of white with orange and black detail, with green luster, $50.00 – 55.00. (2) Creamer with lid, 3¼", swan design, colors of white with orange and black detail, with green luster, $50.00 – 55.00.

From the collection of Mary Gunderson

(1) Black amethyst plate, 9½" across, with sterling silver allover flower design, with outer silver rim and inner silver, $40.00 – 45.00. (2) Toothpick holder, 2", black amethyst glass, frosted satin glass top with silver rim, center is smooth glass with fancy sterling silver design, the flared-out base is frosted satin glass, $35.00 – 40.00. (3) Scepter vase, 7¼", black amethyst glass, top is smooth glass with all-around design of lines and diamonds done in sterling silver, base is straight in the center and flared out on the bottom, frosted satin glass, $80.00 – 85.00.

(1) Vase, 6⅛", black amethyst glass, smooth on the top with sterling silver design, bottom half of vase has appearance similar to old records or lathed or cut grooves, frosted satin, $95.00 – 100.00. (2) Close-up of toothpick holder and scepter vase from page 49.

(1) Open sugar bowl, off-white background with multicolored squares of red, yellow, green, blue, brown allover design, red band around the base, with a red rim, design name Carnival, $40.00 – 45.00. (2) Creamer, off-white background with multicolored squares of red, yellow, green, blue, and brown allover design, red band around the base, with red rim, off-white handle, $40.00 – 45.00.

From the collection of Mary Gunderson

Candy bowl, 4½", green and white with green adventurine, 3 applied pedestal black feet, cased, candy bowl is missing a lid, $45.00 – 50.00.

From the collection of Mary Gunderson

Dresser trinket box, 2" wide x 1⅓" tall glass, amethyst color, enamel painted design on the top and around the base, gold tone metal center band and metal closure, $45.00 – 50.00.

From the collection of Mary Gunderson

(1) Czechoslovakian version of a bride's basket, cased glass, mottled and variegated orange, yellow, and dark brown, silver tone metal basket, bowl is 9" wide x 4" high, in the stand about 8½" high, $85.00 – 90.00. (2) Candlestick, cased glass, black pedestal vase, with orange, yellow, and dark brown, mottled and variegated upper bowl, 2½" high x 4" wide base, $40.00 – 45.00. (3) Melon or flower shape bowl, 7" wide x 4½" high, mottled and variegated, cased glass, done in colors of orange, yellow, and dark brown, matching pieces, $75.00 – 80.00.

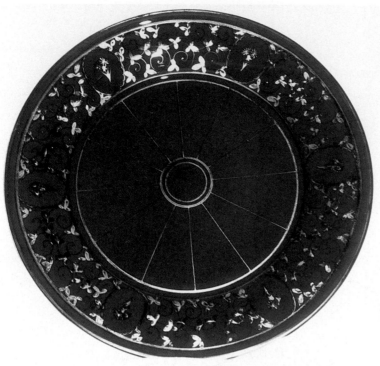

Plate, 10⅜" across, beautiful cobalt blue with wheel spoke center done in sterling silver, band of allover silver design with medallions, 6, each has a design of silver flowers, $65.00 – 70.00.

From the collection of Mary Gunderson

Bowls, pair, 3", cased, red with gold flecks, $80.00 – 85.00 pair.

(1) Powder box, 3½", red with coralene design, $40.00 – 45.00. (2) Bowl, 3", cased, red with black rim, $30.00 – 35.00.

Set, covered pitcher, 12½", 4 glasses, 5", cased, applied clear handle on pitcher, sterling silver bird and trim on pitcher and glasses, $190.00 – 195.00 set.

(1) Vase, 13¼", cased, reds and yellows with clear feet, $60.00 – 65.00. (2) Vase, 11¾", cased, red with fluted black rim, $70.00 – 75.00. (3) Vase, 13½", footed iridescent, $70.00 – 75.00.

(1) Seltzer bottle, 10½", clear, the Waldorf Astoria, $85.00 – 90.00. (2) Seltzer bottle, 12½", clear with wire mesh, $100.00 – 115.00.

(1) Glass figurine, 8¼", doctor in white coat, $220.00 – 225.00. (2) Glass figurine, 9", chemist in white coat and blue pants, $220.00 – 225.00.

(1) Bowl, 3", cased, white with fluted crystal rim, $40.00 – 45.00. (2) Bowl, 3", white with black rim, $30.00 – 35.00. (3) Horn of plenty, 4½", cased, white with clear fluted edge, $65.00 – 70.00.

(1) Vase, 9", cream with mottled red and yellow base, fluted rim, $60.00 – 65.00. (2) Bud vase, 11¾", green with applied purple base, $70.00 – 75.00. (3) Vase, 9", cased, cream with ivory flecks, $150.00 – 160.00.

Compote, 5¾", cased, orange with applied jet feet, $80.00 – 90.00.

Candolier, 9¼", cased, white with gold and cranberry trim and crystal drops, $145.00 – 150.00.

(1) Decanter, 6½", no top, crystal waffle weave, $15.00 – 20.00. (2) Oil and vinegar fish cruet, 8", clear with green tails, $85.00 – 90.00. (3) Lamp base, 5½", crystal, $30.00 – 35.00.

(1) Vase, 4", cut crystal, $25.00 – 30.00. (2) Decanter, 11", amber with painted scene, $65.00 – 70.00. (3) Candleholder, 5", crystal with amber applied clear feet, $15.00 – 20.00.

Vase, 7½", cased, red large squat with reddish purple design, $190.00 – 200.00.

(1) Salt and pepper shakers, 2", cut crystal, $20.00 – 25.00. (2) Salt and pepper shakers, 1¾", crystal with black base, $35.00 – 40.00.

(1) Salt and pepper shakers, 3½", crystal waffle weave, $25.00 – 30.00. (2) Salt and pepper shakers, 2", cut crystal, $25.00 – 30.00. (3) Salt and pepper shakers, 2½", crystal, no tops, $15.00 – 20.00.

(1) Vase, 6", white with gold design and gold rim on bottom, $40.00 – 45.00. (2) Vase, 10", large, amber, $45.00 – 50.00. (3) Vase, 5½", cased ivory with gold design, $35.00 – 40.00,

(1) Vase, 5", cased, orange Roman motif, black painted trim and design, $60.00 – 70.00. (2) Pitcher, 6", orange with white applied handle and cobalt blue threading around rim, $65.00 – 75.00.

(1) Vase, 7½", cased, tomato red with black rim, $55.00 – 60.00. (2) Covered candy dish, 7", cased, clear knob on top and black applied feet, $60.00 – 65.00.

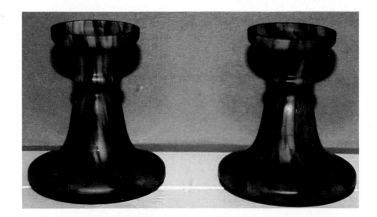

Candlestick holder, 4¼", mottled colors, satin glass, $60.00 – 70.00 pair.

(1) Vase, 7", cased, orange Jack-in-the-pulpit, $45.00 – 55.00. (2) Vase, 6", cased, red with black overlay, $60.00 – 65.00.

(1) Bud vase, 5¼", pink, wide-ribbed with white applied threading, $30.00 – 35.00. (2) Bud vase, 5¼", blue, round with white applied threading, $30.00 – 35.00.

(1) Flower holder, 5½", cased, burnt orange with mottled brown, $80.00 – 85.00. (2) Flower holder, 5", cased, cream with red overlay, $50.00 – 60.00.

(1) Pitcher, 6", smoke colored with applied jet handle and applied red threading, $80.00 – 90.00. (2) Vase, 6¼", cased, round, green with brown, $60.00 – 65.00.

(1) Vase, 6½", cased, pink with applied multicolored red, green, and yellow scallops, pinch bottle type, $185.00 – 190.00. (2) Vase, 6½", cased, pink with applied red and blue scallops, pinch bottle type, $200.00 – 210.00.

Champagne glass, cranberry with crystal stem, 6", $40.00 – 45.00 each.

(1) Basket, 6¼", cased, clear, yellow and red with applied prickly crystal handle, $70.00 – 80.00.
(2) Basket, 9", cased, pink with blue applied handle and blue threading, $160.00 – 165.00.

(1) Decanter, 7½", cased, amber with black top, $40.00 – 50.00. (2) Decanter, 9½", cased, clear with amber and blue panels, $60.00 – 65.00.

(1) Vase, 7", cased, orange with brown overlay bottom, $45.00 – 50.00. (2) Vase, 6¾", multicolored reds, orange, yellow, and brown, $45.00 – 50.00.

(1) Vase, 8½", cased, clear, yellow, blue, and orange, $50.00 – 55.00. (2) Vase, 8¾", cased, clear adventurine, red, yellow, green with fluted black rim top, $75.00 – 80.00.

(1) Vase, 6¼", cased, white, green, and red with cobalt blue applied feet, $55.00 – 60.00. (2) Creamer, 6", cased, pale blue and yellow with cobalt blue rim and applied handle, $80.00 – 85.00.

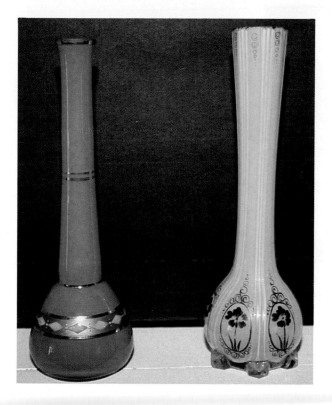

(1) Bud vase, 9½", cased, rose pink with gold trim, $45.00 – 50.00. (2) Bud vase, 10", cased, yellow with clear feet and black decoration, $45.00 – 50.00.

Pitcher, 10¼", amber with green overlay, blue overlay and applied cobalt blue handle and threading, $180.00 – 185.00.

(1) 7-piece bar set, cocktail shaker, 11", 4 glasses, 3", smoke, silver and gold; (2) Ice bucket, 6¼", bitters bottle, 5½", smoke, silver, and gold, $80.00 – 85.00 set.

(1) Vase, 6", cased, pale blue, $40.00 – 45.00. (2) Vase, 6½", cased, green with jet serpentine, $50.00 – 60.00.

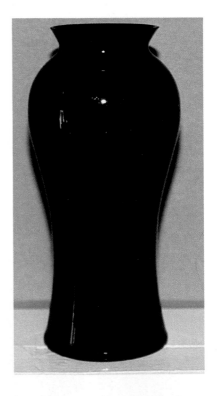

(1) Candy dish, 6", no top, red with mottled green bottom, with applied jet feet, $55.00 – 60.00. (2) Vase, 6¼", cased, red with black rim and bottom and enameled bird and decoration, $55.00 – 65.00.

Vase, 7½", cased, black amethyst, gold paint, $40.00 – 45.00.

(1) Vase, 6", black amethyst, $30.00 – 35.00. (2) Vase, 5", cased, burgundy with white interior and gold rim, $50.00 – 55.00.

(1) Cup, 3½", white with man and woman, $15.00 – 20.00. (2) Cotton ball holder, 2", blue cut glass, $50.00 – 55.00.

(1) Vase, 4½", cased, green, red, and yellow adventurine, $40.00 – 45.00. (2) Vase, 5", cased, pink, white, and brown adventurine, $50.00 – 55.00. (3) Vase, 3", cased, clear, red, and yellow, $25.00 – 30.00.

(1) Vase, 7½", cased, blue with multicolored red, yellow, orange, and green, $45.00 – 50.00. (2) Vase, 8¼", cased, green mottled with variegated yellow and blue, round top and bottom with square body, $45.00 – 55.00.

(1) Vase, 10", cased, cream with blue overlay, blue pedestal bottom, $90.00 – 100.00. (2) Vase, 9½", cased, blue, green, and brownish red, $75.00 – 85.00.

(1) Vase, 8¾", cased, rose, cobalt blue, and yellow overlay, yellow base, $90.00 – 100.00. (2) Vase, 8", cased, rose, green, and orange, white canes, blue detail with red applied threading, $125.00 – 150.00.

(1) Vase, 9¼", pink, cobalt blue overlay with red and blue mottled base, $150.00 – 160.00. (2) Vase, 9¾", cased vaseline with red and yellow canes, blue detail, $180.00 – 185.00.

(1) Bud vase, 8½", cased, blue variegated, $60.00 – 65.00. (2) Bud vase, 8½", cased, yellow with mottled color base, $65.00 – 70.00.

(1) Jack-in-the-pulpit vase, 9½", cased, orange multi-variegated, $80.00 – 85.00. (2) Bud vase, 9¾", cased, red, yellow, blue variegated, $80.00 – 85.00.

(1) Vase, 8½", satin glass, orange, red, yellow, cased, $50.00 – 55.00. (2) Vase, 8", multicolored shades red and yellow with cobalt blue serpentine, $100.00 – 110.00.

(1) Vase, 9", cased, yellow with black serpentine, $45.00 – 50.00. (2) Vase, 8¼", green with black serpentine, $45.00 – 50.00.

(1) Vase, 9¾", cased, orange with black rim, $70.00 – 75.00. (2) Vase, 8¾", red, cased, black applied four footed pedestal base, $70.00 – 80.00.

(1) Vase, 8", cobalt blue mottled, $60.00 – 65.00. (2) Ewer, 8¼", cased, pale blue with fluted top, applied clear crystal handle, $70.00 – 75.00.

(1) Vase, 10¾", cased, turquoise adventurine, mottled, $80.00 – 85.00. (2) Vase, 11¼", cased, ivory with red rick-rack effect, some yellow at base, $115.00 – 120.00.

(1) Vase, 9½", light blue with flecks cream and pink, cobalt blue overlay, pedestal base, $125.00 – 130.00. (2) Vase, 7¾", green with blue and yellow adventurine, applied blue rim, 3 blue applied ball feet, $130.00 – 135.00.

(1) Vase, 8", cased, yellow top with red and brown mottled bottom, $70.00 – 75.00. (2) Vase, 7", cased, yellow with black ruffled rim, $60.00 – 65.00.

(1) Pair vases, 5¾", cased, orange with coralene birds and deco, $60.00 – 65.00. (2) Vase, 6½", cased, orange with applied cobalt blue leaf handles, $70.00 – 75.00.

Pitcher, 8½", pink with amber casing and handle, $40.00 – 50.00 each.

Vase, 8", cased, pink with fluted black rim, $50.00 – 60.00 each.

(1) Vase, 6¾", cased, turquoise with mottled red, $60.00 – 70.00. (2) Vase, 8", vaseline with red, blue, and yellow mottled bottom, $65.00 – 70.00.

(1) Vase, 8½", cased, green with black rim and colored flowers, $50.00 – 60.00. (2) Vase, 8¾", cased, green with vertical black lines, $45.00 – 50.00.

(1) Vase, 8¼", cased, orange and yellow, $45.00 – 50.00. (2) Vase, 9¼", cased, yellow with clear feet and red mottling, $65.00 – 70.00.

(1) Vase, 8", satin glass, red and yellow with brown pedestal base, $70.00 – 80.00. (2) Vase, 7¼", cased, white with orange, red, blue, and green, $50.00 – 60.00.

(1) Vase, 8¼", cased, multicolored with clear feet and applied cobalt blue serpentine, $70.00 – 75.00. (2) Vase, 6¾", cased, orange with cobalt blue applied handles and deco, $85.00 – 90.00.

(1) Vase, 5½", cased, pinch bottle type, red and yellow with applied blue rigerory, $80.00 – 90.00. (2) Vase, 6", cased, red and yellow with applied jet handles, $70.00 – 80.00.

(1) Flower holder, 4", cased, orange with red, $40.00 – 50.00. (2) Flower holder, 4½", cased, orange with black stripes, $40.00 – 50.00.

(1) Powder box, 3", orange with silver birds and trim, $35.00 – 40.00. (2) Covered candy dish, 4½", cased, orange and white with applied cobalt trim and flowers, $60.00 – 65.00.

(1) Vase, 8¼", red with green and brown mottling, cased, applied jet feet, $60.00 – 65.00. (2) Vase, 8¼", red with black, jet rim, cased, $70.00 – 75.00. (3) Vase, 7", orange with brown, cased, $55.00 – 60.00.

(1) Vase, 8", variegated multicolors, cased, applied jet rim, fluted, $60.00 – 65.00. (2) Vase, 9", pink with applied red rim, cased, fluted top, $60.00 – 65.00. (3) Vase, 8½", pink, blue, and white variegated, pedestal base, $65.00 – 70.00.

Vase, 11", yellow cased with applied multi-variegated design, vertical ribbed design in colors, $60.00 – 65.00.

(1) Vase, 8¼", yellow, brown, orange, and red variegated, cased, applied cobalt blue pedestal feet, $70.00 – 75.00. (2) Vase, 8¾", green and red mottled, cased, $65.00 – 70.00. (3) Vase, 8½", red and yellow variegated, with green adventurine, cased, fluted jet rim, $75.00 – 80.00.

(1) Vase, 8", green, cased, glass with applied pink serpentine and leaves, $75.00 – 80.00. (2) Vase, 7½", white cased with red applied handles, $70.00 – 75.00. (3) Vase, 4", flower holder, pink, blue, and white mottled with applied brown base, cased, $60.00 – 65.00.

Set of 6 glasses, green bubble glass with painted scene of Dutch windmills, 4" tall x 2¾" wide, $125.00 – 150.00 set.

7-piece decanter set, 8½" tray, 10¼" decanter, wine-glasses are 4⅛" tall, set is clear glass with applied enameling design, $125.00 – 130.00 set.

(1) Vase, 8¼", orange with blue, cased, satin glass, $60.00 – 70.00. (2) Vase, 9½", orange with brown and blue mottling, cased, $70.00 – 75.00. (3) Vase, 8", orange with jet fluted rim, cased, $45.00 – 50.00.

Square planter, 5½", white cased with blue, yellow, orange, and red mottling on top, applied blue, cobalt base with feet, $75.00 – 80.00.

(1) Pitcher, 4", 3 spouts, yellow and red mottled, cased, applied cobalt handle and rim, unusual, $70.00 – 75.00. (2) Candy jar base, 5½", red and black mottled, cased, applied red pedestal feet, $40.00 – 45.00. (3) Pear-shaped condiment jar, 5¼", orange cased, with multicolored, mottled glass, applied jet top and lines, $65.00 – 70.00.

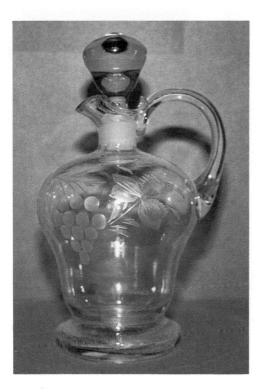

Small green decanter, 8½", deep wheel cut, grape and leaves design, $85.00 – 90.00.

Vase, 7¼", blue mercury glass, $60.00 – 65.00.

Glass barrel with wooden holder, 6" x 6", rough green color with metal spigot, should have 6 small handled shot glasses, $40.00 – 45.00.

(1) Green cased pitcher, 4¾", with cobalt blue applied handle and top decoration, $80.00 – 85.00. (2) Black vase, 8", with variegated colors, cased, satin finish, $70.00 – 75.00. (3) Amber vase, 6", with blue and green, applied base and side decorations, $80.00 – 85.00.

Clear seltzer bottle, 13½", has a metal lattice weave banding, made for Sparklets in New York, $75.00 – 80.00.

(1) Vase, 7⅛", opalescent, very thin, similar to Fry glass, $75.00 – 80.00. (2) Footed bowl, 5⅛", orange applied pedestal feet, bowl is vaseline glass, green, has ribbed design, probably had a lid, candy bowl, $50.00 – 60.00.

(1) Place card holder, 2", clear ribbed pot with green glass leaves, $7.50. (2) Cologne bottle, 3", clear glass with design of enameled flowers all around the base, yellow banded neck and top of stopper, $40.00 – 45.00. (3) Place card holder, 2½", clear ribbed pot with multicolored glass beads, $7.50.

Decanter, 7", rough finish exterior with black stopper and handle, silver fish and plants, 2¾" shot glasses, 4, rough with silver bands, $120.00 – 125.00 set.

Duck decanter and shot glasses in holder, 6¾" x 6", 9" glass-bottom tray, 6 multicolored shot glasses, 3", $150.00 – 155.00 set.

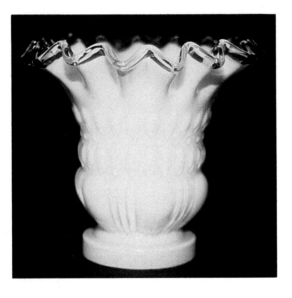

White vase, 5¼", cased, with applied clear fluted rim, $75.00 – 80.00.

(1) Pink vase, 6", cased, with white glass decorations, $60.00 – 65.00. (2) Candleholder, 3½", orange, cased, with applied black jet rim, $40.00 – 45.00.

BUTLER BROS. CATALOG

FANCY BEVERAGE SETS

Orange Decorated
1C-6154 9 piece set, 10x5 in., orange decorated case, raised floral spray, gilt bronze knob and band, inside metal rack with crystal decanter and SIX blown tumblers. 1 set in pkg. **SET (9 pcs) 95c**

Green Frosted Keg
1C6152 — 7 pieces, green frosted keg, 7 in. high, 4 nickel plated hoops, faucet and rack with SIX crystal glasses. 1 set in carton......**SET (7 pcs) 95c**

Floral Embossed
1C-1859—8 piece set, 37 oz. blown decanter, ht 12½ in., SIX 3 oz. footed beverage glasses, ht. 4¾ in., 10⅜ in. deep round tray, floral embossed crystal body, bright tilted-in colors, ruby flowers with green leaves. 4 sets in case. **SET (8 pcs) $1.25**

Blue Frosted Keg
1C-6070—7 piece set, blue frosted keg 7½ in. high, 4 nickeled hoops, faucet and rack, SIX 1 oz. crystal glasses. 1 set in pkg. **SET (7 pcs) $1.65**

Red Decorated
1C-6138—8 piece set, 10½x6½ in., red decorated bell shape glass case, hinged cover, applied illuminated scenic designs, inside metal rack with crystal decanter, SIX blown glasses. 1 set in pkg. **SET (8 pcs) $2.35**

Royal Blue Keg
1C6153—7 pieces, 7 in. high, solid royal blue glass with fired white enameled landscape decoration, 4 nickel plated hoops, gilt band and decorated stopper, nickel plated faucet and rack with SIX blown glasses to match. 1 set in carton. **SET (7 pcs) $1.75**

Frosted Green Glass
1C-6140—8 piece set, 6 in. frosted green glass barrel, nickel plated faucet and 4 hoops, wood stand with legs, SIX 1 oz. handled crystal glasses. 1 set in pkg. **SET (8 pcs) $2.35**

½ Gal. Oak Keg
1C-1253 — 7 piece set, highly polished, nickel plated hoops, fancy bung, wood stand, SIX thin blown 1½ oz. optic glasses. 1 set in carton, 8 lbs. **SET (7 pcs.) $3.25**

Samples from the collection of Mary Gunderson, showing how Czechoslovakian collectibles can be displayed in your home.

Egg beverage set, 9", Mercury crackle glass, $145.00 – 150.00.

From the collection of Mary Gunderson

Egg beverage set, 9", Mercury crackle glass, lid was lifted off rather than hinged, metal tray designed to hold decanter and small set of liquor glasses, $145.00 – 150.00.

From the collection of Mary Gunderson

(1) Non-eggshaped beverage set, 10¼", cobalt blue glass, metal tray inside holds glass decanter and glasses, "Made in Czecho-Slovakia" is stamped in the metal, gold tone metal band with closure, $160.00 – 165.00 set. (2) Egg beverage set, 9", cobalt blue glass with gold painted design or detail on the outside, gold tone metal band with a closure, when opened a metal tray holds a decanter and small glasses, $160.00 – 165.00 set.

From the collection of Mary Gunderson

Beverage set, 9½" tall, upright cobalt barrel, with 8" wide tray, liquor glasses are 2" tall, very fancy design, wide gold band, enamel painted flowers and leaves, also small dots, several gold bands, golden stopper and golden spigot, lovely set, has more detailed elegant painting than most eggs, $155.00 – 160.00 set.

From the collection of Mary Gunderson

From the collection of Mary Gunderson

Egg beverage set, 9", clear glass, painted inside with coralene and beaded glass design on the outside, design that has a person in the center, gold metal center band and closure, inside is a decanter with small glasses, $145.00 – 150.00.

Egg beverage set, 9", clear glass, painted peach inside with beautiful luminescent flowers on the outside done with coralene glass beads, $150.00 – 155.00.

(1) Egg beverage set, 9", from page 84, when opened has decanter in metal tray with small glasses, has metal band and metal closure, $145.00 – 150.00. (2) Egg beverage set, 9", clear glass, painted orange inside, remains of the coralene glass beads, in design of flowers with gold painted accents, gold tone metal band with closure, when opened has decanter with small glasses, $145.00 – 150.00.

From the collection of Mary Gunderson

From the collection of Mary Gunderson

(1) Egg beverage set, 9", clear glass outside, painted red inside, coralene glass beads in the design of a bird on a branch with berries on the other branches, has black trim, gold tone band and closure, when opened has metal tray that holds a decanter and small glasses, $150.00 – 155.00. (2) Egg beverage set, 9", clear glass on the outside, painted light blue on the inside, the design on the outside done with coralene glass beads, pink and gold tulips with gold leaves, trim in black and gold, gold tone metal band with closure, when opened has a metal tray that holds a decanter and small glasses, $150.00 – 155.00.

Left: Upright beverage barrel, 8", cobalt blue glass, green drop-in stopper, design of enamel painted flowers and ferns, has metal spigot, $90.00 – 95.00.

Right: Upright beverage barrel, 8½", clear frosted overshot glass barrel, clear glass drop-in stopper, 4 metal bands and spigot, $65.00 – 70.00.

From the collection of Mary Gunderson

From the collection of Mary Gunderson

Horizontal beverage barrel, 8" long x 5¼" wide x 6¼" high, orange cased glass, has silver trim with center design of grape leaves, missing stand and hardware, $80.00 – 85.00.

(1) Closed Czech egg decanter set, 9", blue interior, outside design of a coralene bird with painted flowers and golden design and band, $150.00 – 155.00. (2) Closed Czech egg decanter set, 9¼", mauve interior, outside design of a coralene bird with nuts, also gold painted leaves and band, $150.00 – 155.00.

(1) Open Czech egg decanter set, blue interior, gold metal closure and decanter holder, 7¼" tall decanter with 6 very small 1" tall liquor glasses, $150.00 – 155.00. (2) Open Czech egg decanter set, mauve interior, gold metal closure and decanter holder, 6" tall decanter with 6 very small 2" tall liquor glasses, $150.00 – 155.00.

PERFUMES AND COLOGNES

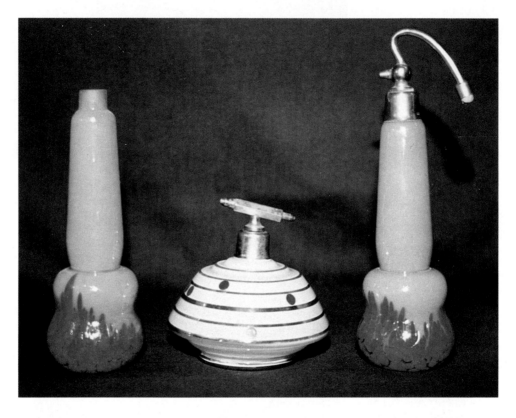

(1) Green cased glass atomizer, 5¾", with an overlay of mottled red at the base, $75.00 – 80.00. (2) Atomizer, 4", blue cased base, with a design of silver bands, also has painted enamel red spots, gold tone metal sprayer, $50.00 – 55.00. (3) Green cased atomizer, 5¾", glass, with an overlay of mottled red at the base, gold tone metal sprayer head, $75.00 – 80.00.

(1) Drop stopper, 3¾", clear crystal, intaglio cut, flowers and leaves, stopper intact, $45.00 – 50.00. (2) Miniature cologne pinch bottle, 1¼", with screw-on cap, clear bottle with painted enamel design, with gold detail, $20.00 – 25.00. (3) Perfume stopper, 2", round faceted cut crystal, $20.00 – 25.00.

(1) Perfume, 5½", with stopper, clear with deep cut design on the base, deep cut panel design on the stopper, $80.00 – 85.00. (2) Perfume, 6½", with stopper, deep cut ridged design on the base, intaglio cut rose design on the stopper, open center, $85.00 – 90.00. (3) Atomizer, 2½", clear glass with ridged design on base, with painted enamel design in blue and white, gold tone metal sprayer with yellow rubber bulb, $40.00 – 45.00.

(1) Atomizer base, 3¾", pale green painted glass bottle, has painted enamel flowers around the top, black banded trim, gold tone metal top, $40.00 – 45.00. (2) Perfume, 4¼", with stopper, clear base with deep cut design, unusual bottle shape, green drop stopper also has deep cut design, $105.00 – 110.00. (3) Atomizer, 3¾", pale yellow bottle with blue, gold, and black design, gold tone metal top, with blue rubber bulb, $40.00 – 45.00.

(1) Atomizer base, 5", golden metal top, glass bottle is amber iridescent with frosted top with black trim, and painted enamel design, $40.00 – 45.00. (2) Atomizer base, 5", gold tone metal top, glass bottle is rainbow iridescent color with design of painted enamel flowers around the top, $40.00 – 45.00. (3) Atomizer base, 5", gold tone metal top, glass bottle is amber iridescent with frosted top with black trim, and painted enamel design, $40.00 – 45.00.

(1) Perfume bottle, 5¼", with stopper, clear glass pressed design of ribbing on 4-sided bottle and on the stopper, $45.00 – 50.00. (2) Atomizer, 3", clear with ridged design, has square design with Xs in the center on both sides, top sprayer is gold tone metal, $65.00 – 70.00. (3) Atomizer base, 3", clear glass with deep cut prism design, heavyweight, gold tone metal top, $45.00 – 50.00.

(1) Atomizer, 8", orange cased bottle, with mottled colors on the base, metal top with the sprayer, goldish rubber and fabric bulb and line, $80.00 – 85.00. (2) Atomizer, 8", bright orange cased bottle, black pedestal base, metal top and sprayer, goldish rubber and fabric bulb and line, $80.00 – 85.00.

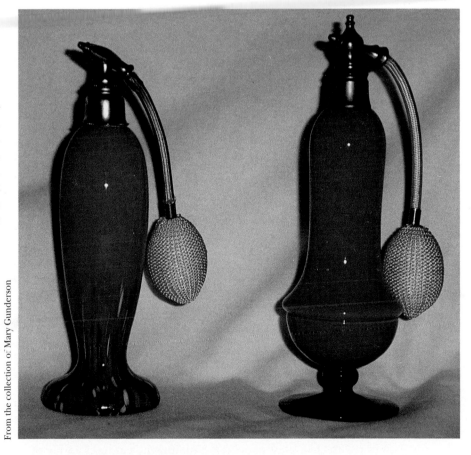

From the collection of Mary Gunderson

From the collection of Mary Gunderson

(1) Covered vanity dresser jar, 3¼" high x 4" wide, clear glass with allover design of painted enamel daisies, multicolored, knob has silver on the top, $40.00 – 45.00. (2) Small hinged vanity jar, probably for trinkets, clear glass with enamel painted design on the lid, white flower with orange center and white leaves, hinge and closure are bronze colored metal, $30.00 – 35.00.

(1) Blue crystal atomizer, 2", has square hobnail design on the base, has silver tone top, metal sprayer, $35.00 – 40.00. (2) Cobalt blue atomizer, 5", has gold design of leaves and bands, has gold tone top, metal, $50.00 – 55.00. (3) Blue crystal atomizer, 4¾", 6-sided base, has pressed design, has gold tone metal top and sprayer, with clear glass panel top, with intaglio cut roses and leaves, crystal, $65.00 – 70.00.

(1) Clear crystal perfume, 6", 4-sided base with deep cut diamond design, 4-sided drop stopper, also has deep cut diamond design, $175.00 – 180.00. (2) Clear crystal perfume, 2½", small triangle shape base, deep cut allover design on the base, clear crystal drop stopper, with intaglio cut design of flowers and leaves, $90.00 – 95.00. (3) Crystal perfume, 6½", 4-sided clear crystal base, deep cut allover design on the base, blue crystal drop stopper, triangular sided with intaglio cut design of flowers and leaves, $180.00 – 185.00.

Perfume bottle, 9¼", blue crystal with deep ridge cut design, tall drop stopper, blue with deep cut scallop design on triangle style stopper, $270.00 – 275.00.

(1) Blue crystal atomizer, 3¼", has deep cut ridge design on base, gold tone metal sprayer, $70.00 – 75.00. (2) Blue crystal atomizer, 7½", has deep cut ridge design on base, vertical, gold tone metal sprayer with yellow rubber and fabric bulb, $80.00 – 85.00. (3) Blue crystal atomizer, 2¾", has deep cut square ridge design, gold tone metal sprayer with yellow rubber and fabric bulb, $70.00 – 75.00.

(1) Crystal atomizer, 2¾", pink, base is 3-sided with 2 triangles per side, has deep cut allover ridge design, silver tone metal top and sprayer, the top has a pink stone set in the sprayer, $50.00 – 55.00. (2) Crystal atomizer, 3", pink base with allover cut design, gold tone metal top and sprayer, very top is a horizontal crystal panel with intaglio cut flower design, $90.00 – 95.00. (3) Perfume bottle, 4", crystal, angular cut clear pink crystal base, pink crystal drop stopper with prism cut, $65.00 – 70.00.

(1) Amethyst perfume, 5", crystal, 6-sided base with deep cut acid etched design on base, prism cut amethyst drop stopper, $65.00 – 70.00. (2) Smoke color crystal perfume, 6½", deep cut allover design on the base, prism cut smoke color drop stopper, $60.00 – 65.00. (3) Amethyst perfume, 5¾", crystal, deep thumbprint design all around base, triangular amethyst drop stopper with deep cut design in the center, $65.00 – 70.00.

Miniature perfume bottle, 2¾", crystal, pink base with cut and shaped design of a butterfly, embellished with gold filigree with pink and white mottled polished stones, set in the middle with a pearl, clear prism cut crystal drop stopper, $135.00 – 140.00.

Miniature perfume bottle, 2", clear crystal base with shaped design, embellished with gold filigree, set with cut amethyst stones, painted with white enamel, screw-on metal lid with glass drop stopper, very top of lid set with rib cut amethyst stone, $135.00 – 140.00.

Miniature perfume bottle, 2½", clear crystal base completely encased in metal filigree, enamel painted flowers and leaves, set with pink faceted glass stones, metal screw-on lid, with glass drop stopper, with a clear faceted stone, $85.00 – 90.00.

(1) Miniature perfume bottle, 2½", clear crystal base with pressed allover design, metal screw-on lid, with glass drop stopper, peach colored faceted stone on the very top with 2 gold chains with 2 peach cone drop stones, $55.00 – 60.00. (2) Miniature perfume bottle, 1½", amethyst crystal cut base, missing stopper, $40.00 – 45.00.

(1) Miniature perfume bottle, 2¾", crystal, black 4-sided base with clear 4-sided drop stopper, $110.00 – 115.00. (2) Crystal amber atomizer, 2", deep cut allover design on base, gold tone metal top and sprayer, pale yellow rubber and fabric spray bulb, $50.00 – 55.00. (3) Miniature perfume bottle, 2½", crystal, clear allover design on base, metal screw-on lid with glass drop stopper, faceted amber stone on top, $35.00 – 40.00.

Miniature perfume bottle, 2", round, orange glass bottle textured, with applied glass flowers and leaves, silver tone metal bottle neck and silver glass knob with silver glass drop stopper. Shown in original box, $150.00 – 155.00.

(1) Green crystal perfume, 6½", pedestal base has ridge design with layered top, deep cut wheel etched design in center, oval green crystal drop stopper, with intaglio design of flowers and leaves, $175.00 – 180.00. (2) Crystal perfume, 4¼", base is clear with a black diamond design in the center, with cut design, base is multi-sided, clear drop stopper is prism cut crystal, $140.00 – 145.00. (3) Crystal perfume, 5¾", green pedestal base, allover deep cut design of diamonds, clear crystal drop stopper is tree shaped with deep cut design of tree branches, $160.00 – 165.00.

(1) Amber crystal perfume, 4¾", 6-sided base with 3 ridge design around the base, ridge design on amber drop stopper, stopper is also 6-sided, $55.00 – 60.00. (2) Pale yellow crystal perfume, 3¼", rectangle base with deep cut allover design, clear crystal drop stopper, has faceted prism design, $80.00 – 85.00.

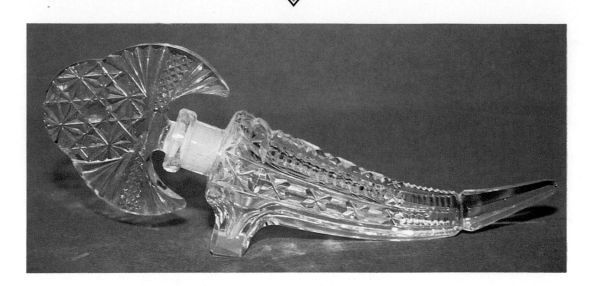

Crystal perfume, 6¼", base is very pale yellow, horn of plenty design, set on its side, allover deep cut design, has 2 feet at the front, clear crystal drop stopper has deep cut design, very rare, $250.00 – 255.00.

Glass atomizer, 6½", cased, cobalt blue with multicolored overlay on the base, gold tone metal top and sprayer, black rubber and fabric bulb, with black tassel, $110.00 – 115.00.

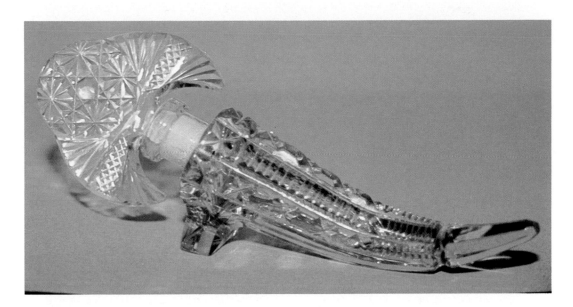

Crystal perfume, 6¼", horn of plenty design, base is light blue, set on its side, allover deep cut design, has 2 feet at the front, clear crystal drop stopper has deep cut design, very rare, $250.00 – 255.00.

Glass atomizer base, 6¼", clear glass with hand-painted enamel scene, Middle Eastern desert oasis with palm trees with camel and man done in black silhouette, silver tone metal top, $145.00 – 150.00.

Glass atomizer, 4¼", yellow, orange cased glass with black pedestal base, hand-painted enamel scene, homestead with trees done in black, brown, and white, $145.00 – 150.00.

(1) Vanity bottle, 6", crystal cranberry with clear base, "peroxide" deep etched on the front, clear faceted prism cut on round ball drop-in stopper, $50.00 – 55.00. (2) Vanity bottle, 2¾", crystal cranberry and clear cotton ball holder, "cotton" deep etched on the front, lid missing, $35.00 – 40.00. (3) Vanity bottle, 6", crystal cranberry with clear base, "mouth wash" deep etched on the front, clear faceted prism cut on round ball drop-in stopper, $50.00 – 55.00.

(1) Dresser set, 4¼", cologne bottle, clear base with frosted bands around the sides, with bands of gold, top of bottle is frosted, neck of the bottle and stopper also frosted, with gold band on neck and stopper, $35.00 – 40.00. (2) Powder dish, 4" across, cased glass base and lid, yellow, with applied handle of glass, pink rose and green leaves, $40.00 – 45.00. (3) Dresser set, 5¼", cologne bottle, clear base with textured top, has 4 gold bands around bottle with 1 around rim, clear round drop-in stopper with gold at the top, $35.00 – 40.00.

(1) Vanity bowl, 1½", probably for jewelry or trinkets, green glass, heavyweight, crystal, $20.00 – 25.00. (2) Vanity bowl, 2", powder dish or trinket bowl, pink crystal base, has layered ridge design, lid is a mirror on one side with a metal design on the other side, collapsible handle is the same as the base, pink crystal with deep cut design, lightly frosted, silver metal band and hinge, $65.00 – 70.00.

(1) Dresser set, 4¼", cologne bottle, clear with allover blue enamel painted stars, blue bands around the neck and rim of bottle, round blue enamel ball stopper, $35.00 – 40.00. (2) Dresser set, 4", powder dish with lid, allover painted enamel blue stars on clear base and lid, blue band around base and rim, round blue enamel ball stopper, $35.00 – 40.00. (3) Dresser set, 4½", cotton jar, clear glass with blue enamel painted stars all over base, blue bands around neck and rim, large round blue enamel ball knob, $35.00 – 40.00.

(1) Dresser set, 6", cologne bottle, clear base with multicolored enamel flowers, painted, has a silver band around the base and rim, clear round drop-in stopper with silver on the top, $35.00 – 40.00. (2) Dresser set, 4¾", cologne bottle, clear base with multicolored enamel painted flowers, has a red band at the base and rim, clear round drop-in stopper with red on the top, $35.00 – 40.00. (3) Same as in (1), $35.00 – 40.00.

(1) Dresser set, 4¾", cologne bottle, clear glass with bubble design, clear round ball stopper, $35.00 – 40.00. (2) Dresser set, 3¾", powder dish with lid, clear glass with bubble design on base and lid, clear glass round ball handle, $35.00 – 40.00. (3)Same as in (1), $35.00 – 40.00.

(1) Dresser set, 3½", powder dish and lid, clear base with frosted panel around the center, gold band around the base and the top, also blue band, lid has frosting with painted enamel flowers around center and on top of knob, blue band around edges, $40.00 – 45.00. (2) Dresser set, 4½", cologne bottle, frosted band with blue and gold bands around the base and side, top is frosted with painted enamel band around the center, blue band around neck, glass knob with bands and flowers on the top, $40.00 – 45.00.

Bohemian decanter, 10", 2 glasses 6", ruby and clear with deer and hunting dog, $200.00 – 210.00 set.

Moser decanter 8", amber, $50.00 – 75.00.

Moser cranberry bowl and plate 2½", enameled allover design, $225.00 – 250.00 set.

JEWELRY AND BUCKLES

(1) Bracelet, 7½", silver tone setting, large faceted crystal stones, $40.00 – 45.00. (2) Bracelet, 8" double row of blue faceted stones, large stone clasp closure, $40.00 – 45.00. (3) Necklace, 17½" golden chain and setting, 1 large rectangle with 10 smaller ones, glass, clear with cut-in design, $70.00 – 75.00. (4) Necklace, 15", silver tone chain and setting, large faceted crystal stones, $50.00 – 55.00. (5) Choker, 13", child's necklace, golden setting with double row of clear faceted rhinestones, $50.00 – 55.00.

(1) Golden chain, 17", with red glass beads, small round with 3 oblong beads, 1 large teardrop center bead drop, $50.00 – 55.00. (2) Silver and black choker, 16", metal chain with metal balls and flat design pieces, black flat glass alternating pieces, unusual design, $50.00 – 55.00. (3) Child's choker, 12", pink and white mottled glass, flat beads, highly polished, $50.00 – 55.00. (4) Light green faceted glass beads, 16", graduated sizes, closure has green stone in the center, $45.00 – 50.00. (5) Golden chain with setting, 18", large blue faceted center stone, smaller emerald cut stone above, $65.00 – 70.00.

(1) Flapper beads, 35", 1920s, faceted red and pink glass beads, 4 sizes, round, oval, and oblong shapes, $60.00 – 65.00. (2) Flapper beads, 35", 1920s, crystal and jet glass faceted beads, round, teardrop, oblong, and oval shapes, $60.00 – 65.00. (3) Multicolored agate and glass beads, 28", oblong, oval, and round shapes, $60.00 – 65.00. (4) Polished coral with jet glass beads, 31", round shape, $55.00 – 60.00.

(1) Small and large red glass beads, 16", center glass bead has cut-in design, $50.00 – 55.00. (2) 4 shades of blue stones, 15", glass, faceted, $50.00 – 55.00. (3) Black faceted and circle glass beads, 17", golden chain with double strand, $55.00 – 60.00. (4) Green faceted crystal glass beads, 14", graduated sizes, $50.00 – 55.00. (5) Green and black glass beads, 15" round, circle, and semicircle that fit together, very unusual, $55.00 – 60.00.

(1) Light and dark green glass faceted beads, 19½", assorted shapes and sizes, oblong center drop, $65.00 – 70.00. (2) Necklace, 18", red, black, white, and clear faceted glass beads, rhinestones and black center drop stone, $65.00 – 70.00. (3) Choker, 15", large and small blue and white swirled glass beads, with light blue and tan round and flat glass beads, blue stone closure, $50.00 – 55.00. (4) Golden chain and setting, 20", round red glass beads, 1 large oval cabochon center stone, Victorian era, $80.00 – 85.00. (5) Golden chain and setting, 20½", red, orange, and burgundy glass beads with black center drop with chevron design glass, $70.00 – 75.00.

(1) Pearl necklace, 44", continuous, no closure, $45.00 – 50.00. (2) Necklace, 28", crystal aurora borealis, faceted beads, $50.00 – 55.00. (3) Pearl necklace, 23", with closure, $50.00 – 55.00. (4) Navy blue and white glass beads, 33", assorted shapes, some with designs, $50.00 – 55.00.

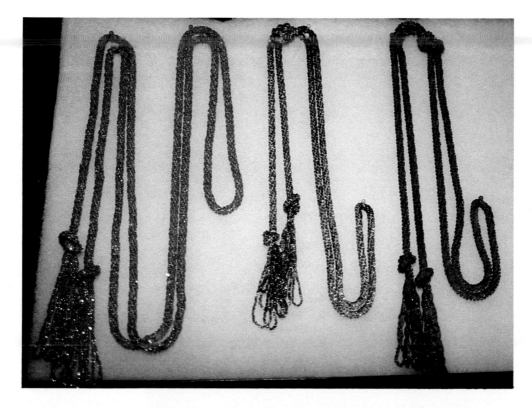

(1) Flapper beads, 82", 1920s, pink, worn as a necklace or belt, $40.00 – 45.00. (2) Flapper beads, 46", 1920s, gold, necklace, $40.00 – 45.00. (3) Flapper beads, 48", 1920s, red, necklace, $40.00 – 45.00.

(1) Necklace, 28", orange branch coral, small jet glass beads, unusual shapes of the coral, $50.00 – 55.00. (2) Necklace, 15", golden color chain and settings, light amber square cut glass stones, $50.00 – 55.00. (3) Necklace, 17½", silver filigree chain and setting, jet glass beads, assorted shapes and sizes, $70.00 – 75.00. (4) Necklace, 15½", golden chain with gold and silver setting, faceted amethyst glass stones, 1 large oval faceted center stone, $70.00 – 75.00.

(1) Necklace, 16½", golden chain and setting, glass faceted beads, faceted rhinestones, $55.00 – 60.00. (2) Necklace, 16½", golden chain and setting, large emerald cut amber stones, $60.00 – 65.00. (3) Bracelet, 7", gold tone settings, double row of red faceted rhinestones, large stone clasp closure, $45.00 – 50.00. (4) Necklace, 16½", very fine silver chain and holders, 6 glass faceted amber beads, pointed shape, 1 large amber teardrop-shaped center stone, $55.00 – 60.00. (5) Necklace, 13½", choker style, gold tone setting and chain, triple row center design, clear faceted smaller stones with 3 graduated sizes of center stones, $65.00 – 70.00.

(1) Coral, glass, and amber faceted beads, 30½", with brown rods, $50.00 – 55.00. (2) Golden chain and setting, 26", with tan and orange glass cameo, $50.00 – 55.00. (3) Golden chain and settings, 16", with 5 blue cut glass stones, $50.00 – 55.00. (4) Light and dark blue glass beads, 38", $50.00 – 55.00.

(1) Graduated coral cylindrical beads, 17", $45.00 – 50.00. (2) Multi-shaded, brown striped, 15", feather shape glass beads, with tan square cut beads, $50.00 – 55.00. (3) Multi-pink and white striped feather shape glass beads, 18", with cream color square cut beads, $50.00 – 55.00. (4) Blue and light yellow round glass beads, 16½", $45.00 – 50.00. (5) Shaped coral glass beads with smaller white and clear round glass beads, 17", $45.00 – 50.00.

(1) Small black beads with red shaded triangle glass beads, 17", $40.00 – 45.00. (2) Crystal tube beads and faceted round beads, 23", gold color chain with 2 faceted triangle crystal drops, $50.00 – 55.00. (3) Cylindrical turquoise and black beads, 16", star design is cut into the black beads, $35.00 – 40.00. (4) Glass faceted beads, 26½", black with aurora borealis, $40.00 – 45.00. (5) Red glass beads, 18", 1 large rectangle with graduated size beads on a golden chain, $60.00 – 65.00.

(1) Green and white, mottled beads, 16", glass, graduated sizes, $45.00 – 50.00. (2) Big and small blue-green glass beads,14", $45.00 – 50.00. (3) Yellow and white, faceted, glass beads, 14", with stone closure, $45.00 – 50.00. (4) Light blue square and triangle glass beads, 14½", $45.00 – 50.00. (5) Silver flowers with blue swirl glass beads, 17", $45.00 – 50.00.

(1) Red and black faceted, graduated sizes, glass beads, 19½", with clear spaces, $45.00 – 50.00. (2) Yellow and white, mottled, graduated size beads, 16¼", $45.00 – 50.00. (3) Amber and black, 19¼", graduated size beads, $45.00 – 50.00. (4) Clear faceted, and red glass beads, 17", $50.00 – 55.00. (5) Wooden and glass beads, 18½", assorted colors, $45.00 – 50.00.

Row A: (1) Garnet pin, 2", gold tone setting, pheasant, set with faceted garnets, $60.00 – 65.00. (2) Garnet pin, 1½", gold tone setting, fish, set with faceted garnets, $60.00 – 65.00.
Row B: (1) Garnet ring, 1" across, silver setting, polished agate center, surrounded by 2 rows of faceted garnets, $60.00 – 65.00. (2) Garnet ring, 1" across, silver setting, polished agate center, surrounded by 2 rows of faceted garnets, $60.00 – 65.00.
Row C: (1) Garnet pin, 1", golden setting, surrounded and set with faceted garnets, butterfly, $55.00 – 60.00. (2) Garnet ring, ¼" across, golden setting, set with a single faceted garnet, $20.00 – 25.00. (3) Garnet ring, ¼" across, golden setting, set with a single faceted garnet, $20.00 – 25.00. (4) Garnet pin, ¾", golden setting, surrounded and set with faceted garnets, butterfly, $55.00 – 60.00.
Row D: (1) Garnet pendant, ¾" across, golden setting, religious figure, with "Prazske Jezulatko" inscribed, surrounded by faceted garnets, $40.00 – 45.00. (2) Garnet pendant, ½" across, golden setting, Prague castle, surrounded by faceted garnets, $40.00 – 45.00. (3) Garnet pendant, ½" across, golden setting, set with faceted garnets, $40.00 – 45.00.

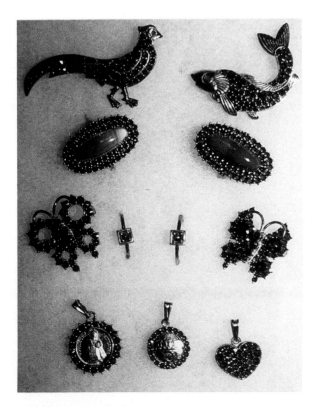

Row A: Pin, 1½", golden setting with blue shades of light and dark glass beads, $30.00 – 35.00.

Row B: (1) Pin, 2", silver tone setting, glass faceted rhinestones, $40.00 – 45.00. (2) Pin, 2¼", black background with tapestry center, golden setting, red and blue small faceted stones, $40.00 – 45.00.

Row C: (1) Pin, 2¼", design made with assorted colors and shapes of wooden beads, small multi-colored glass beads, $30.00 – 35.00. (2) Pin, 2", small pale green beads with golden leaves, 4 blue-green faceted glass stones, $30.00 – 35.00.

Row D: Pin, 1¾", golden setting with blue-green faceted stones, 4 rectangle blue moonstones, $30.00 – 35.00.

Row A: (1) Pin, 2¼", golden setting with large and small faceted blue-green stones, $60.00 – 65.00. (2) Bug pin, 2", golden setting, 1 large blue faceted center stone, multicolored faceted small stones, $60.00 – 65.00.

Row B: (1) Butterfly, 1½", golden setting, multicolored faceted stones, $35.00 – 40.00. (2) Pin, 1½", golden open style setting, multicolored and multi-shaped faceted stones, $40.00 – 45.00. (3) Lavelier pin, 1½" x 3", golden chain and setting with blue-green faceted stones, assorted sizes, enameling, $65.00 – 70.00.

Row C: (1) Pin, 1½", golden setting with pink faceted stones, $60.00 – 65.00. (2) Pin, 1¼", golden setting, 1 large faceted sapphire center stone, with pearls, small blue-green faceted stones, enameling, $50.00 – 55.00.

Row A: (1) Pin, 2", golden setting, amber faceted pear-shaped glass stones, $40.00 – 45.00. (2) Pin, 1½", bar style, with enamel design under high gloss finish, $20.00 – 25.00. (3) Pin, 1¼", basket of fruit, bronze color setting, red glass basket, fruit and beads, $25.00 – 30.00.

Row B: Pin, 1", golden setting with enameling, blue-green faceted stones with pearl accents, $35.00 – 40.00.

Row C: (1) Pin, 1½", golden color, road runner shape setting, turquoise color glass beads, $25.00 – 30.00. (2) Pin, 2", bronze color, fancy curved setting, multi-colored and sized faceted stones, $30.00 – 35.00. (3) Pin, 1½", silver horse with enameling, $25.00 – 30.00.

Row D: (1) Pin, 1", plastic Scottie, black with movable head, $15.00 – 20.00. (2) Pin, 2", gold tone fancy setting with silver tone accents, $20.00 – 25.00.

Row A: (1) Buckle, 2¼", glass with cut design, blue color, $25.00 – 30.00. (2) Buckle, 1¾", glass with cut design, amber color, $20.00 – 25.00.

Row B: Pin, 2", silver tone spider setting with red glass large center stone, $20.00 – 25.00.

Row C: (1) Buckle, 1½", bronze color metal, filigree setting, set with faceted rhinestones, $25.00 – 30.00. (2) Buckle, 1", glass, small, light brown with triangle design pressed in, $15.00 – 20.00.

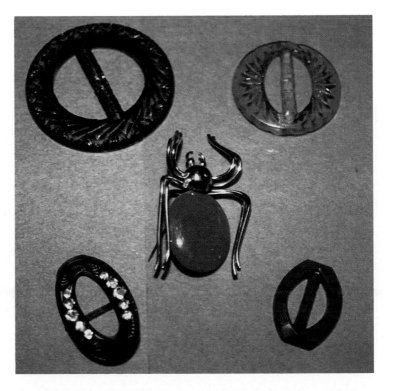

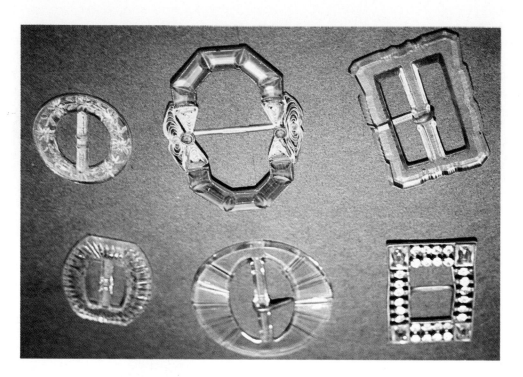

(1) Belt, 32", woven red saran, 2¼" buckle, golden setting with celluloid red rainbow design, $35.00 – 40.00. (2) Belt, 24", blue velvet, 2½" buckle, black glass with gold and silver design, $30.00 – 35.00. (3) Belt, 32", black velvet, 2" buckle, clear glass with pressed design, $35.00 – 40.00.

Row A: (1) Buckle, 2¼", golden setting with large and small faceted rhinestones, $40.00 – 45.00. (2) Buckle, 2½", clear glass with cut-in design of lines, $35.00 – 40.00. (3) Buckle, 1¾", clear glass with fancy cut design, $25.00 – 30.00.
Row B: (1) Buckle, 1¾", clear glass with fancy cut edges, $25.00 – 30.00. (2) Buckle, 3", fancy golden setting, large faceted amber stones, $50.00 – 55.00. (3) Buckle, 1½", clear glass with flower design all-around, $20.00 – 25.00.

Row A: (1) Buckle, 3", green glass with gold accents, $25.00 – 30.00. (2) Buckle, 2¼", celluloid, brown, tan, and rust design, $25.00 – 30.00.
Row B: (1) Buckle, 3", glass, gold color with gold accents, $25.00 – 30.00. (2) Buckle, 2½", metal design with green celluloid, $25.00 – 30.00.
Row C: (1) Buckle, 2¾", golden setting with celluloid center of yellow, brown, and pink design, $30.00 – 35.00. (2) Buckle, 2¼", fancy golden setting, faceted rhinestones, $40.00 – 45.00.

Row A: Drop earrings, 1½" long, screw type back, gold tone setting, 1 large center moonstone with multicolored faceted stones, $35.00 – 40.00.
Row B: (1) Drop earrings, 1" long, screw type back, gold tone setting, 2 large pink faceted center stones, lower stone is surrounded by smaller pink faceted stones, $25.00 – 30.00. (2) Button style earrings, ½" across, screw type back, blue glass with small pearls in the center, $15.00 – 20.00.
Row C: (1) Golf clubs pin, 2¼" long, silver tone metal, $20.00 – 25.00. (2) Pin, 2" long, gold tone shape and setting of an open-winged butterfly, decorated with gold filigree, gold beads, pink faceted stones and enameling, $40.00 – 45.00.

Row A: Earrings, 1½", clip back, marquis cut amber stones, pear-shaped green stones, $35.00 – 40.00.

Row B: (1) Earrings, 1", screw back, dark red and red faceted stones, $35.00 – 40.00. (2) Earrings, 1", screw back, light and dark pink faceted stones, $35.00 – 40.00.

Row C: Earrings, ¾", screw back, enamel flowers, with blue faceted stones, $25.00 – 30.00.

Row D: (1) Earrings, 1", screw back, blue-green pear shaped faceted stones, $35.00 – 40.00. (2) Earrings, 1", screw back, red pear-shaped and round faceted stones, $35.00 – 40.00.

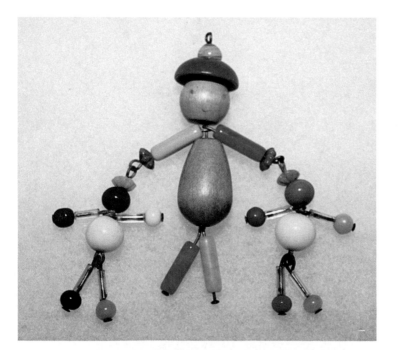

Wooden and glass man, 3", 2 children made of glass beads, 1½" tall, a whimsical piece, unusual, $20.00 – 25.00.

Row A: (1) Ring, 1" across, gold tone setting and band, faceted dark amber center stone, $70.00 – 75.00. (2) Ring, 1" across, gold tone filigree setting and band, large faceted pink center stone, surrounded by small round faceted pink stones, $80.00 – 85.00.

Row B: (1) Ring, ¼" across, golden setting and band, faceted yellow moonstone in center, $20.00 – 25.00. (2) Ring, ¼" across, golden setting and band, faceted light amethyst stone, $20.00 – 25.00.

Row A: (1) Earrings, 1", pierced, silver black Bohemian glass beads, $25.00 – 30.00. (2) Earrings, 1", pierced, black Bohemian glass beads, $25.00 – 30.00.
Row B: Earrings, 1", pierced, black Bohemian iridescent glass beads, $25.00 – 30.00.

(1) Purse, 3¾" x 5½", white cloth bag, has finger holder on end, design of white seed beads with gold, zipper closure, $20.00 – 25.00. (2) Purse, 4½" x 9", white cloth bag, design of ivory, white and gold seed beads, black and silver leaf tube beads, hand holder on back, zipper closure, $40.00 – 45.00.

Purse, 9½" x 7½", gold frame top, handle and closure, black satin bag, covered with a design of black sequins with ropes of small black glass beads, along with several large black beads, $65.00 – 70.00.

Purse, 5" x 6¼", black cloth bag, design of multicolored and multi-size wooden beads, handle made of beads, zipper closure, $40.00 – 45.00.

Purse, 4½" x 7½", black cloth bag, drawstring closure, design of black and silver small glass beads, $60.00 – 65.00.

Purse, 5½" x 7½", red cloth bag, drawstring closure, allover design made with red glass seed beads, $60.00 – 65.00.

(1) Purse, 4¼" x 7", black cloth body, rose and leaf design, black and clear seed beads, clear and black tube beads, hand holder on back, zipper closure, $35.00 – 40.00. (2) Purse, 3¾" x 5½", black cloth bag, design of clear and black seed beads, zipper closure, 2 beaded handles, $35.00 – 40.00.

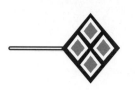 

Perfume lamp, 6", mushroom-shaped, satin finish, enamel design on outside in colors of red, blue, and yellow flowers with green leaves, electric, $120.00 – 125.00.

Lamp, 6", multicolored, mushroom-shaped, clear feet, $220.00 – 230.00.

Basket lamp, 9½", glass flowers and beads with beaded handle, $300.00 – 325.00.

Lamp, 9½", green and oxblood, $200.00 – 210.00.

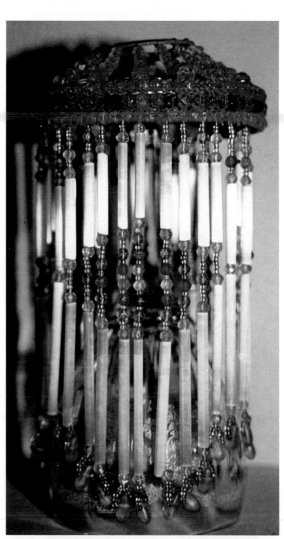

Small beaded lampshade, 8", top is done in small faceted pink glass beads, the drops are made of pink, gold, red, and clear faceted glass beads, along with pink glass tubes, the bottom beads are oblong satin glass beads. Very rare to find intact, $75.00 – 80.00.

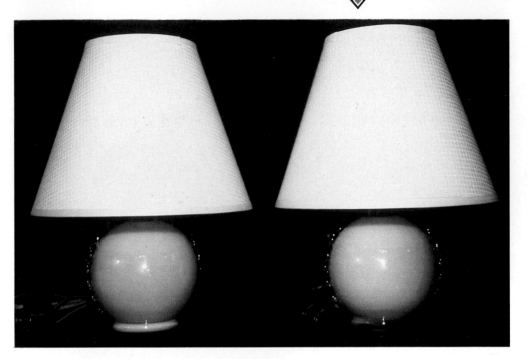

Pair of lamps, 4½" tall without shades, balls are white cased glass, applied orange rigaree down both sides of each lamp, probably vanity lamps, $50.00 a pair.

Lamp, single, 24¼" tall, hurricane style with candlestick type base, brass base, fittings, switch and globe holder, clear chimney, top is white glass ball with painted enamel flowers and leaves, multicolored. Center is white cut back to blue with enamel painted flowers and leaves. The bottom is white cut back to pink with enamel painted flowers and leaves, $275.00 – 300.00.

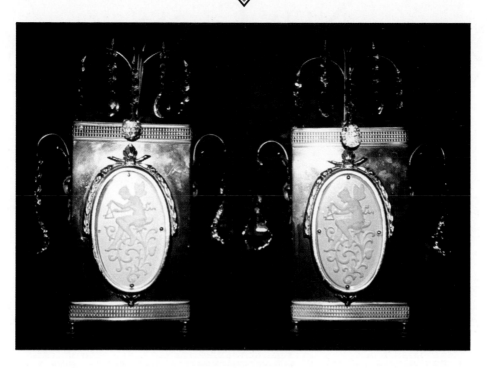

Lamps, pair, 16¼" tall each, metal case of purplish brown color, top and bottom bands are brass, accents and feet also are brass, large faceted drops at the top and sides, smaller crystals are above the large drops, these are also cut and faceted. Center of the lamp is an oval crystal with an intaglio cut of a fairy, she is playing a triangle while sitting on flowers, $450.00 – 500.00 a pair.

Lamp, 7" across x 7" high, 6-sided metal frame and base, set on 6 metal feet, gold tone color, amber and clear faceted crystal beads in design around the center. The top of the lamp is covered with assorted glass fruit and nuts, very bright colors, also berries and leaves. Lamp has 2 handles, 1 on either side, the lamp is electrified. Very hard to find with the top design intact, $550.00 – 600.00.

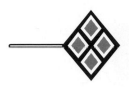 

(1) Czech egg, hand painted, purple base with allover beige design, $20.00. (2) Czech egg, hand painted, red base with allover white design, with center flower, $20.00. (3) Czech egg, hand painted, black base with allover white design, with berries in the center, $20.00. (4) Czech egg, hand painted, brown base with allover beige design of flowers and leaves, $20.00. (5) Czech egg, hand painted, green base with allover white design, with chicken in the center, $20.00. Made in Slovakia.

(1) Czech egg, brown enamel with golden braid around the center, gold geometric string design, $20.00. (2) Czech egg, green enamel with golden braid around the center, gold geometric string design, $20.00. (3) Czech egg, red enamel with golden braid around the center, gold geometric string design, $20.00. (4) Czech egg, blue enamel with golden braid around the center, gold geometric string design, $20.00. (5) Czech egg, pink enamel with golden braid around the center, gold geometric string design, $20.00.

Decanter with 4 wineglasses, clear crystal with ribbed design, 14" tall decanter, 6½" tall wineglasses, $50.00 – 55.00.

Decanter with 4 liquor glasses, amber colored glass with gold trim, 11¼" tall decanter, 2¾" glasses, $60.00 – 65.00.

Apple-shaped jar, 5¼", clear iridescent glass with yellow and green mottling on the top, clear stopper with long dropper, scent bottle by Czech glass blower, Vernon Brejcha of the United States, $145.00 – 150.00.

Decanter with 4 liquor glasses, blue glass with gold trim, 14½" tall decanter with 3" tall glasses, $60.00 – 65.00.

7-piece decanter set, 9½" tall hand-blown crystal decanter, hand etched with a design of roses and leaves done in gold, set of 6 small 2¼" tall glasses, same design on glasses as decanter, $65.00 – 70.00.

Closed Czech egg decanter and glass holder, 8½", done in the shape of a basketball, golden metal closure with chains on either side, color is brown with black detail, golden metal stand, $60.00 – 65.00.

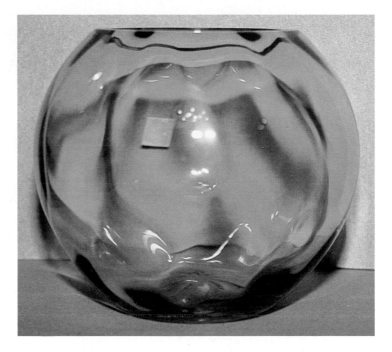

Rose bowl, 5", blue crystal, has swirl design in the glass, $40.00 – 45.00.

Vase, 8¼", lead crystal, has allover diamond pattern with frosted flowers, $60.00 – 65.00.

Bell, 5¼", cobalt blue glass, gold overlay in the center and the top, with a gold band, enamel flower design in the center, $25.00 – 30.00.

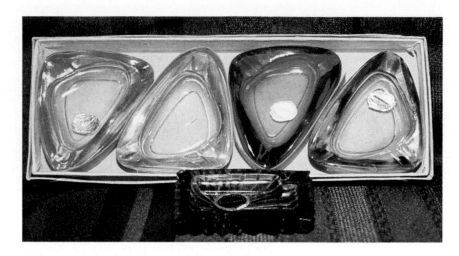

(1) Set of 4 ashtrays in box, 2", pink, blue, amber, and green, $20.00 – 25.00 set. (2) Oblong ashtray, 2¾" x 2", amber, $15.00 – 17.00.

Champagne flutes, 8¼", set of 4, clear crystal with a ribbed design in the glass, $45.00 – 50.00 set.

(1) Crystal shell with pearl, 1¾" x 2¼", $40.00 – 45.00. (2) Vase, 9¾", crystal, clear and frosted, $35.00 – 40.00.

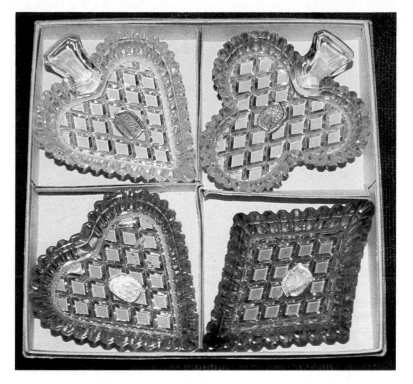

Set of 4 ashtrays in box, card suits, blue, green, pink, and amber, $25.00 – 30.00 set.

Set of 4 ashtrays in box, crystal, card suits, $20.00 – 25.00 set.

UNCOMMON ITEMS, TOYS, AND MISCELLANEOUS

Bar set, 12", decanter with small glasses, white, cased with green, several Grecian scenes with enameling, $150.00 – 160.00.

(1) Humidor, 8¼", girl in a bag, $340.00 – 345.00. (2) Bank, 3", lady's face, glazed, $160.00 – 165.00. (3) Vase, 9¼", pottery, pinkish rose with flowers and leaves, $70.00 – 75.00.

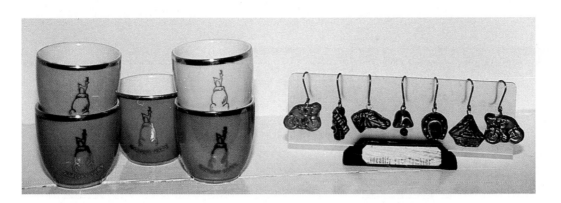

(1) 5 small cups, 1¾", from Karlovy Vary Spa, various colors, $3.00 – 4.00 each. (2) Drink markers with stand, markers glass, $50.00 – 55.00 set.

Place card holders, ¾", flower baskets, 7, $60.00 – 65.00 set.

Figurine, 2¼", Madonna, frosted crystal, $85.00 – 90.00.

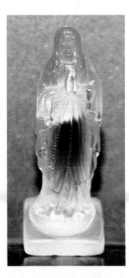

(1) Dresser box, 4½", porcelain, 6-sided, pale orange and yellow base and lid, allover basket weave design, braided band at the top and bottom of the base, knob is a rose on the lid, raised painted flower design across the front, colors of pale green, pale blue, and blue-green, $45.00 – 50.00. (2) Dresser box, 4½", porcelain, 6-sided, pale center design of blue-green, blue, and light green on raised design of flower garland, dark orange and yellow base and lid, allover basket weave design, braided band at top and bottom of the base, knob on the lid is a rose, $45.00 – 50.00.

(1) Shaker, 3¼", girl with umbrella, colors of yellow with green, orange, and brown detail, Erphila, $35.00 – 40.00. (2) Shaker, 3", boy with squeezebox, colors of blue with yellow, red, and brown detail, Erphila, $35.00 – 40.00.

(1) Candleholder, 6", square base with raised 4-corner design, finger hole handle, white background with blue rim and also blue trim, small flower design above larger flower design in the middle on the front, $35.00 – 40.00. (2) Vase, 3¼", oblong with unusual handles, bright yellow with gold bands at the top center and the base, center design of lady and man in silhouette of black, $45.00 – 50.00. (3) Same as candleholder in (1), $35.00 – 40.00.

(1) Salt and pepper set, 1½" tall each, pair of clear glass shakers have clear glass lids, $25.00 – 30.00. (2) Salt and pepper set, 2" tall each, has 2½" red glass tray, pair of cut crystal clear shakers have red glass tops, $45.00 – 50.00.

(1) Sugar shaker, 6", cut crystal prism design with sterling silver shaker lid, $55.00 – 60.00. (2) Salt dips, 2" across, clear glass with starburst design, hexagon shape, $10.00 – 15.00 each.

(1) Photo frame, 4" tall x 3" wide, gold tone metal with design, has pink, green, red, and yellow glass flowers, $20.00 – 25.00. (2) Photo frame, 3½" tall x 2½" wide, bronze tone metal with design, with dark and light faceted amber glass stones on 4 sides, $15.00 – 20.00.

Circle of glass beads, 10½" wide, probably used on the bottom of a lampshade, design of red tubes, with orange, green, clear, black, and dark amber faceted beads, $30.00 – 35.00.

Beaded hanging basket, 26" long x 8" wide, card holder or letter holder, design of flowers is done in glass beads in colors of black, turquoise, pink, gold, yellow, green, white, and clear, hanger is made of black tubes and pink, very intricate work, $75.00 – 80.00.

(1) Picture frame, 4" x 2¾", silver with gemstones, $15.00 – 20.00. (2) Treasure box with key, 1½" x 3", $35.00 – 40.00.

(1) Chandolier crystal, 1½", $10.00 – 12.00. (2) Numbered crystal game piece, 1", $20.00 – 25.00.

(1) Chicken egg holders, 3", pottery, brown with beige detail, 1 pair, $25.00 – 30.00 pair. (2) 9 salt dips, ¾" high x 1½" across, mottled green with green leaf border, pink flower and leaf center, $6.00 – 8.00 each.

Set of 12 place card holders, 1" tall, glass pot with glass flowers and leaves, colors of pink, red, orange, yellow, and blue, $55.00 – 60.00 set.

2 sets of place card holders, 6 in a set, 2½" tall, round prism cut base with glass flowers and leaves, flower colors of white, pink, red, light blue, blue, orange, and yellow, $45.00 – 50.00 per set of 6.

(1) Spoon, 5", fancy design handle and edge of the bowl, black and silver setting, porcelain center of a Delft Dutch boy, $35.00 – 40.00. (2) Spoon, 5", fancy design handle and edge of the bowl, black and silver setting, porcelain center of a blue Delft sailboat, $35.00 – 40.00. (3) Spoon, 5", fancy design handle and edge of the bowl, black, and silver setting, porcelain center of a scene of multicolored flowers, $35.00 – 40.00. (4) Spoon, 5", fancy design handle and edge of the bowl, black and silver setting, porcelain center of a Delft city scene, $35.00 – 40.00.

(1) Spoon, 5", silver setting, fancy handle and edge of bowl, porcelain center and top of spoon with fruit, $35.00 – 40.00. (2) Spoon, 5", silver setting, fancy handle and edge of bowl, porcelain center and top of spoon with birds, $35.00 – 40.00. (3) Spoon, 5", silver setting, fancy handle and edge of bowl, porcelain center and top of spoon with fruit, $35.00 – 40.00.

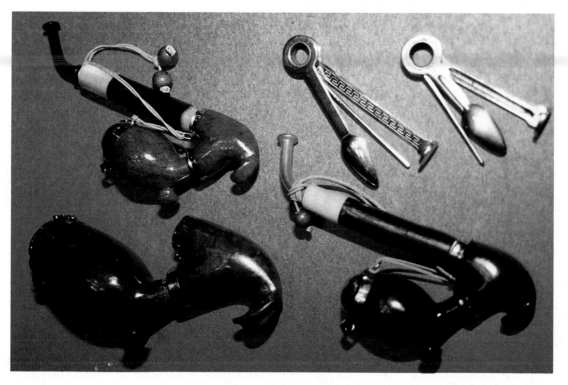

Row A: (1) Pipe, 3" wooden bowl with 3½" stem with beads, silver tone bowl lid and collars, $100.00 – 110.00. (2) 3¼" pipe tamper with rod and spoon, silver tone with design, $20.00 – 25.00. (3) 2½" pipe tamper with rod and spoon, silver tone, $15.00 – 20.00.
Row B: (1) Pipe, 5" wooden bowl with silver tone lid and collar, $60.00 – 65.00. (2) Pipe, 3" wooden bowl with 4" stem, with beads, silver tone bowl lid and collars, $90.00 – 100.00.

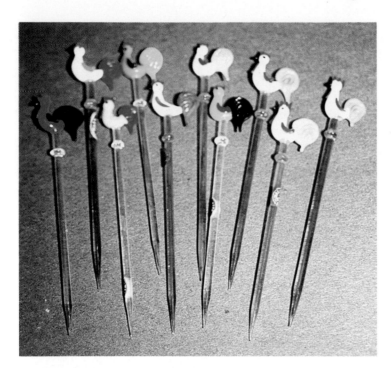

Set of 10 glass fruit holders for drinks, all different shapes and colors of glass chickens. Each is 4" long, sold as a set. Very unusual and hard to find, $65.00 – 70.00 set.

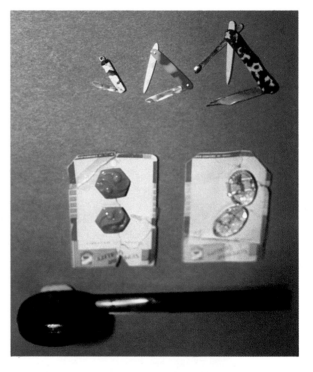

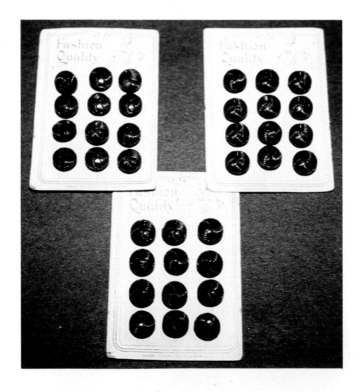

Row A: (1) 1 card of glass buttons, ⅜" each, cut-in design, color of button is amber, $10.00 – 12.50. (2) 1 card of glass buttons, ⅜" each, cut-in design, color of buttons is green, $10.00 – 12.50.

Row B: 1 card of glass buttons, ⅜" each, cut-in design, color of buttons is amethyst, $10.00 – 12.50.

Row A: Tape measure, 1¾" diameter, Mechanics Pal, metal, 71" length, $25.00 – 30.00.

Row B: (1) Card of buttons, clear glass with cut-in design, size of buttons 1" each, $5.00 – 10.00. (2) Card of buttons, green glass with pressed design, size of buttons ¾" each, $5.00 – 10.00.

Row C: (1) Knife, 2", burgundy and ivory celluloid, 1 blade, 1 pick, 1 spoon, $30.00 – 35.00. (2) Knife, 1¼", red and yellow celluloid, 1 blade, 1 pick, $25.00 – 30.00. (3) Knife, 1", ivory, black, and turquoise celluloid, 1 blade, $20.00 – 25.00.

(1) Rubber doll, 8½", blue dress and vest, white blouse and apron, red hat, shoes, and tie, carrying a black basket, $30.00 – 35.00. (2) Hot water bottle, 10", bear shape with drum and collar, orange color with red, blue, white, yellow, and black detail, very unusual, $30.00 – 35.00. (3) Rubber doll, 7", white dress or skirt and blouse and apron with white hat, black shoes with red bows, red vest and red detail, holding a black heart, $25.00 – 30.00.

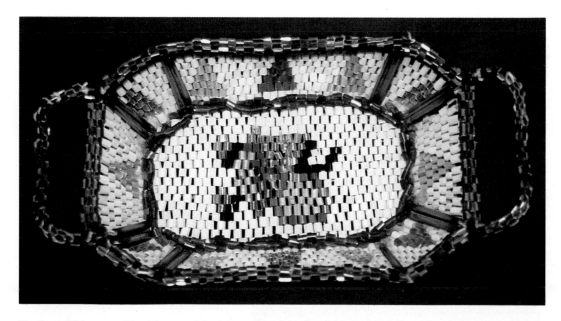

Basket, 8" long x 5" wide, card holder, glass beads, design done in red, pink, green, blue, yellow, and black, borders and handles done in bronze beads and glass tube beads, $55.00 – 60.00.

Child's chamber pot, shown with original pink mottled box, with metal carry handle, 3¼", pink porcelain over metal, enamel painted white dog with red bow and tongue, black trim in the center, pristine condition, never used, $60.00 – 65.00.

Mug, 3¾", porcelain over metal, white interior and handle, dark blue rim, center design of pansy and leaves in blue, yellow, and green with white. Mug has orange shading on top and bottom, $25.00 – 30.00.

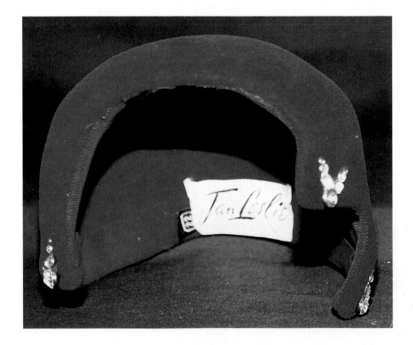

Wool felt hat, bright pink, side view.

Wool felt hat, 5" across, rhinestone design and trim, tonak, bright pink, Jan Leslie, custom design, unusual, $15.00 – 20.00.

Chamber pot, 3½" high, child's, porcelain over metal, light blue, $25.00 – 30.00.

Poppy seed grinder, 9" tall x 3½" wide, metal, blue, metal feeder bowl, wooden handle end, $240.00 – 245.00.

Toy, 5" long tractor with a 6" long trailer, made of tin, brightly colored, clockwork wind up motor, with key, working gear box, 3 forward and 1 reverse, working handbrake and working steering, $30.00 – 35.00.

(1) Miniature charm, 1", blue monkey, sitting, glitter eyes, $20.00 – 25.00. (2) Clear glass frosted owl, 1", glitter eyes, golden collar with hanging stone, $20.00 – 25.00. (3) Miniature charm, 1", green and black glass monkey, tiny glitter eyes, wire collar with hanging stone, $20.00 – 25.00. (4) Miniature charm, ¾", black cat, sitting, tiny glitter eyes, wire collar with hanging stone, $20.00 – 25.00. (5) Miniature charm, 1", blue glass frosted bulldog, red glass eyes, metal collar with red glass bead, $20.00 – 25.00. (6) Miniature charm, 1", green glass frosted owl with red glass eyes, gold tone metal collar with red hanging stone, $20.00 – 25.00.

Green glass frosted bull-dog, 2", miniature charm, rhinestone eyes, golden metal collar with hanging stone, $30.00 – 35.00.

Toy, 6½", clown with metal crank music box, wooden with bright enamel paint, $35.00 – 40.00.

Toy soldiers, set of 6, wooden with bright enamel paint, 4¾" tall each, $25.00 – 30.00 set .

Pop-up book, 12¾" x 9", *Day of the Bison Hunt*, cover closed with Indian chief, book printed in Prague by the Artia Company, circa 1960s, $25.00 – 30.00.

Toy, violin, 11" long, metal with wood, brown with copper and black detail, $40.00 – 45.00.

Day of the Bison Hunt, open, all pages have scenes like these, very well done book, very colorful.

Pop-up book, 12¾" x 9", *Christopher Columbus*, cover closed with ship's wheel, book printed in Prague by the Artia Company, circa 1960s, $25.00 – 30.00.

Glass bells, set of 6, Christmas ornaments, 2" tall, colors of red, gold, blue, and silver with white and pink, gold, green, and silver with white, box marked "Czechoslovakia," $40.00 – 45.00 set.

Christopher Columbus, open, all pages have very colorful scenes like these, very well done.

(1) Large Santa head, 4", has white coralene beard, mustache and hat, $95.00 – 100.00. (2) Standing Santa, 4½", in costume, has white coralene on white areas, $95.00 – 100.00. (3) Pink strawberry, 2", has white coralene top, $25.00 – 30.00. (4) Small standing Santa, 2½", bright colors, $25.00 – 30.00.

Glass ornaments, set of 4, 3" balls, circa '50s or '60s, colors of red, white, and blue. Each has a glitter design, $35.00 – 40.00 set.

Ornaments, 1½" diameter each, glass, set of 7, possibly the '50s or '60s, primary colors of green, gold, red, and silver. Each has a design of silver glitter on the outside, $50.00 – 55.00 set.

(1) Calendar headers, 12½" long x 6" wide, cardboard, scenic picture with birds, done in very bright colors, $10.00 – 12.50. (2) Calendar headers, 13½" long x 7½" wide, cardboard, scenic picture of ships on the water with birds, originally done with very bright colors, $10.00 – 12.50.

(1) Linen tablecloth, 50" x 50", green, orange, and white design, $25.00 – 30.00. (2) Linen napkins, set of 6, each 11½" x 12", colors of beige, red, green, yellow, and black in a design, $25.00 – 30.00.

Embroidered tea towel, pale green background with black, green and beige border with fringe edge, $7.50 – 10.00.

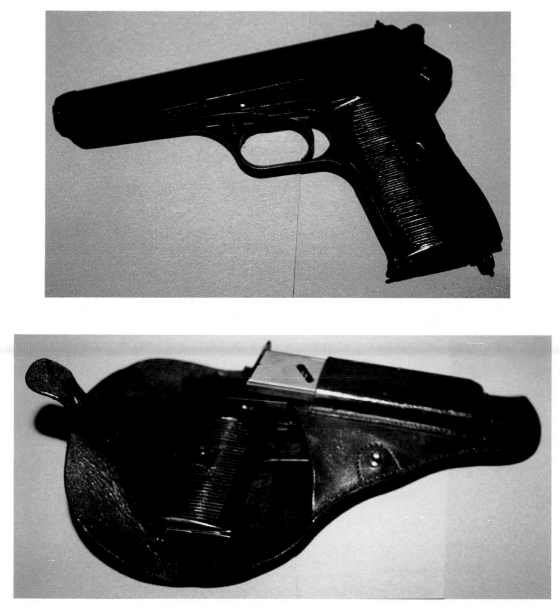

Czechoslovakian handgun, 7.62 x 25mm, model 52, made from 1952 through 1970. It operates on recoil, semi-automatic fire only, weighs 2.31 lbs. and barrel is 4.71 inches long. Clip is removable 8 round box magazine with a muzzle velocity of 1600 F.P.S., shown with its leather holster, $145.00 – 150.00 gun, holster, and clip.

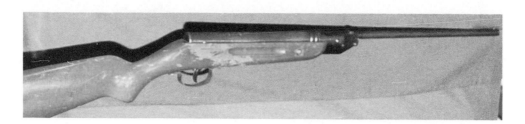

Seavia, "618", air rifle, 14" barrel, 35½" overall length, has open sights, all hardwood stock, made in Czechoslovakia, $75.00 – 80.00.

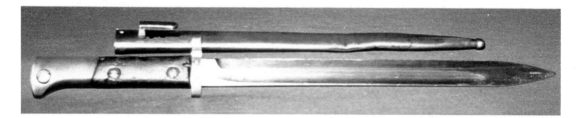

Bayonette, fits an 8mm Czechoslovakian army rifle as shown in Book 1. The blade is 11¾" long and 17" overall length, sheath is 12½" long, $30.00 – 35.00.

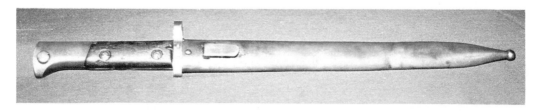

Bayonette, shown in its sheath.

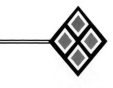

GLOSSARY

Adornment: To add on ornamentation.

Adventurine: Glass that has a glitter effect especially in the light.

Atomizer: Device used to reduce liquid to a fine spray.

Cased: To incase in a second layer. Also called double glass.

Clear Glass: No color, see through.

Coralene: Small glass beads applied and adhered to outer enamel design.

Crystal: Highest quality of glass.

Cut Glass: Glass with a design or shape obtained by cutting, grinding, and polishing.

Decoration: To add on an adornment to make an object fancier.

Drop Stopper: A long narrow glass rod with a tiny ball on the end. It is attached to the bottle top and reaches near the bottle bottom to apply perfume.

Enamel: A very shiny paint, used for design on glass surface.

Frosted: Surface of the glass is made to look frosty.

Intaglio Cut: The design is cut below the surface, giving an image in relief.

Iridescent: A rainbow play of colors on the glass surface.

Jet: A glossy dark black glass.

Mottled: A spotty or blotched design in one or more colors.

Opalescent: Milky, iridescent that has delicate changeable colors.

Opaque: Solid glass that cannot be seen through.

Ornamentation: An added detail such as metal, jewels or enameling on items.

Overlay: A decorative and contrasting design on top of a plain one.

Paint: Applied color, or to decorate with colors.

Relief: Vividness or sharpness of an outline due to contrast.

Satin Glass: Very dull finish from either being sand blasted or dipped in acid. Has a very smooth silky feel.

Serpentine: An applied design on glass in the form of a serpent or snake.

Stopper: A stubby short piece on a lid of a bottle used to apply perfume.

Varicolored: Two or more colors used in glass.

Variegated: Marks with different colors in spots, streaks or stripes.

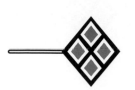 # MARKS

On the next few pages, many of the marks known to us are shown. A number of marks for glass and jewelry are very small when compared to the pottery marks. There are still more marks that we do not show. Collectors know the value difference of a piece that is marked and one that is not. But it is only fair to emphasize that some are not marked. A great majority will be marked, but some, depending on how they got here, will not be marked.

In 1887 or 1888, the United States required imported goods to be marked as to their point of origin. In the year 1921, this was changed to be more specific as to the country, such as "Nippon" which then became "Japan."

Besides exporting to our country, Czechoslovakia also exported to a great many other countries, including England. The other countries were not as stringent as to the markings of the imports, as was the United States. Many items were exported unmarked. From these countries, many pieces came to the United States with immigrants and by tourists traveling abroad. It is also good to note here that many items were sold in pairs with only one piece of the pair marked.

Some pieces made around the 1920s have no etching or stamp marks except for a sticker. This proves that some items were imported with only a sticker. Once the sticker was removed, the piece became unmarked.

Collectors need to bear in mind that not all pieces are marked and each piece must be judged on its own merit. An astute collector will know a Czechoslovakian collectible by its style even if it is not marked.

The marks below are found on pottery, porcelain, semi-porcelain, and china.

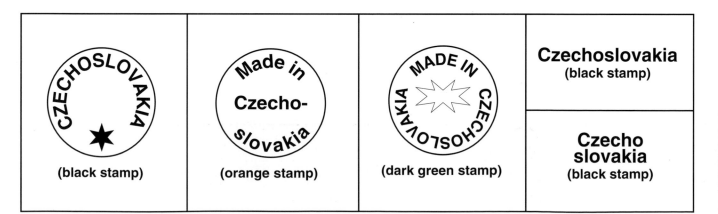

The marks below are found on pottery.

R
CZECHOSLOVAKIA
hand-painting

Handpainted
C
CZECHOSLOVAKIA

CZECHO SLOVAKIA
W
green stamp

REGISTERED
CELEBRATE
MADE IN CZECHOSLOVAKIA

czechoslovakia • made in czechoslovakia
**blue stamp
with acorn**

KERAMIA
**red sticker
with gold printing & design**

• MADE IN •
CZECHOSLOVAKIA
**black sticker
with tan printing & design**

18 57
N
T
CZECHOSLOVAKIA
REMBRANDT
handpainted
green & gold

UNION
T
Czecho-Slovakia

CZECHO- SLOVAKIA
**green stamp
on back with**
Angelica Kauffman
on front

Made in
Czecho-Slovakia
green stamp

CARNIVAL
CZECHOSLOVAKIA

**MADE IN
CZECHOSLOVAKIA**

brown mark

The marks below are found on pottery, porcelain, semi-porcelain, and china.

MADE IN CZECHOSLOVAKIA
(dark green stamp)

Registered
(brown stamp)

CZECHOSLOVAKIA
(black stamp)

EST. 1886 ERPHILA CZECHO-SLOVAKIA
(reddish-brown stamp)

UNION **K**
(dark green stamp)

Czecho-Slovakia
(reddish-orange stamp)

CZECHOSLOVAKIA
(green stamp)

VICTORIA CHINA
CZECHOSLOVAKIA
(black stamp)

Made In Czechoslovakia
(dark blue-green stamp)

Made In Czechoslovakia
(reddish-orange stamp)

RK G MADE IN CZECHOSLOVAKIA
(orange stamp)

TRADE MARK "CORONET" Czechoslovakia Registered
(black stamp)

MADE IN PV CZECHOSLOVAKIA
50034
(black stamp)

Czechoslovakia
Hand - painted
(black stamp)

G CELEBRATE REGISTERED CZECHOSLOVAKIA
(green stamp)

CCC ROYAL BLUE
CZECHOSLOVAKIA
(black stamp)

P.A.L.T.
CZECHO - SLOVAKIA
(light green stamp)

H and-painted
DITMAR URACH
Made in Czecho-slovakia
(black stamp)

EPIAG
Czechoslovakia
(black stamp)

MZ ALTROhLAU CMR CZECHOSLOVAKIA
(green stamp)

VICTORIA
Czecho — slovakia
(black stamp)

The marks below are found on pottery, porcelain, semi-porcelain, and china.

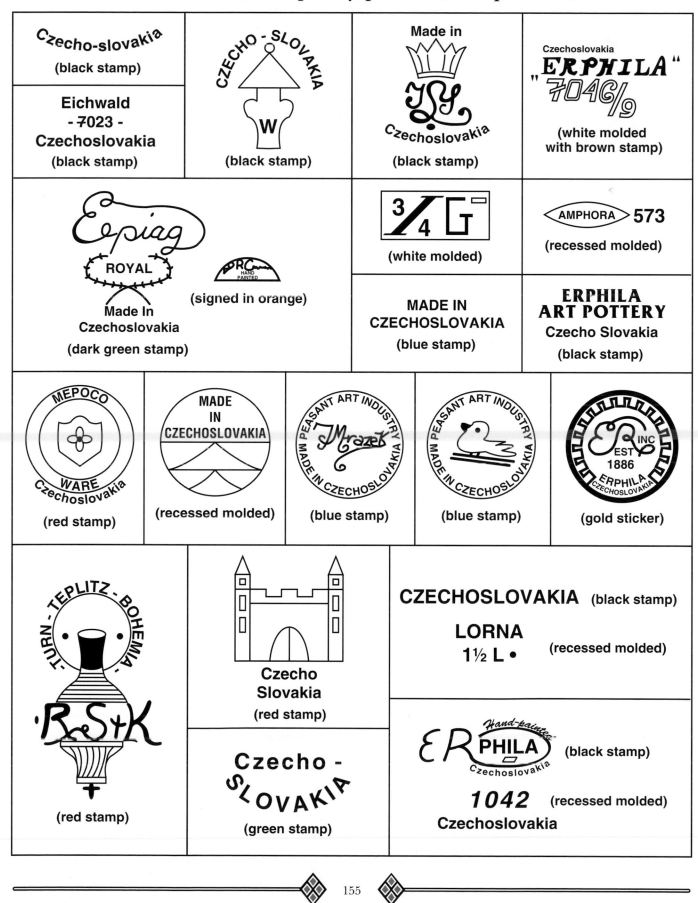

Czecho-slovakia
(black stamp)

Eichwald
- 7023 -
Czechoslovakia
(black stamp)

CZECHO - SLOVAKIA
W
(black stamp)

Made in
JSY
Czechoslovakia
(black stamp)

Czechoslovakia
"ERPHILA"
7046/9
(white molded
with brown stamp)

Eepiag
ROYAL
Made In
Czechoslovakia
(dark green stamp)

PRC
HAND PAINTED
(signed in orange)

3/4 G
(white molded)

MADE IN
CZECHOSLOVAKIA
(blue stamp)

AMPHORA 573
(recessed molded)

ERPHILA
ART POTTERY
Czecho Slovakia
(black stamp)

MEPOCO
WARE
Czechoslovakia
(red stamp)

MADE
IN
CZECHOSLOVAKIA
(recessed molded)

PEASANT ART INDUSTRY
JMrazek
MADE IN CZECHOSLOVAKIA
(blue stamp)

PEASANT ART INDUSTRY
MADE IN CZECHOSLOVAKIA
(blue stamp)

ER EST 1886 INC
ERPHILA
CZECHOSLOVAKIA
(gold sticker)

TURN - TEPLITZ - BOHEMIA -
RStK
(red stamp)

Czecho
Slovakia
(red stamp)

Czecho -
SLOVAKIA
(green stamp)

CZECHOSLOVAKIA (black stamp)

LORNA
1½ L •
(recessed molded)

ERPHILA
Hand-painted
Czechoslovakia
(black stamp)

1042 (recessed molded)
Czechoslovakia

The marks below are found on glass.

beige sticker
with red printing & design

back stamp

back stamp

red with
gold printing & design

gold sticker
with black printing & design

yellow sticker
with silver printing & design

light orange sticker
with silver printing & design

The marks below are found on glassware, perfume bottles, and other glass items.

Made in Czecho-slovakia (black stamp)	Made in Czecho-slovakia (black stamp)
Made in Czecho-slovakia (silver stamp)	CZECHO-SLOVAKIA (silver stamp)
MADE IN CZECHO-SLOVAKIA (silver stamp)	

CZECHO-SLOVAKIA (silver stamp)

Made in Czechoslovakia (sticker)

Made in Czecho-slovakia (sticker)

Made In Czechoslovakia (white acid etched)

CZECHO-SLOVAKIA (white acid etched)

Made in Czecho slovakia Mco Mco (black & white sticker)

MADE IN CZECHO-SLOVAKIA (white acid etched)

Made in Czecho slovakia (black & white sticker)

Made in Czecho slovakia (red & white sticker)

Czecho Slovakia (white acid etched)

Czecho Slovakia (black script stamp)

CZECHOSLOVAKIA (white acid etched)

TCHECOSLOVAQUIE (acid etched)

Czechoslovakia (white acid etched)

Moser (acid etched)

Moser MADE IN CZECHOSLOVAKIA (gold sticker)

CZECHOSLOVAKIA (silver stamp)

CZECHOSLOWAKIA (black stamp)

Made in Czechoslovakia (white acid etched)

Czechoslovakia (white acid etched)

The marks below are found on metal items, jewelry, and purses.

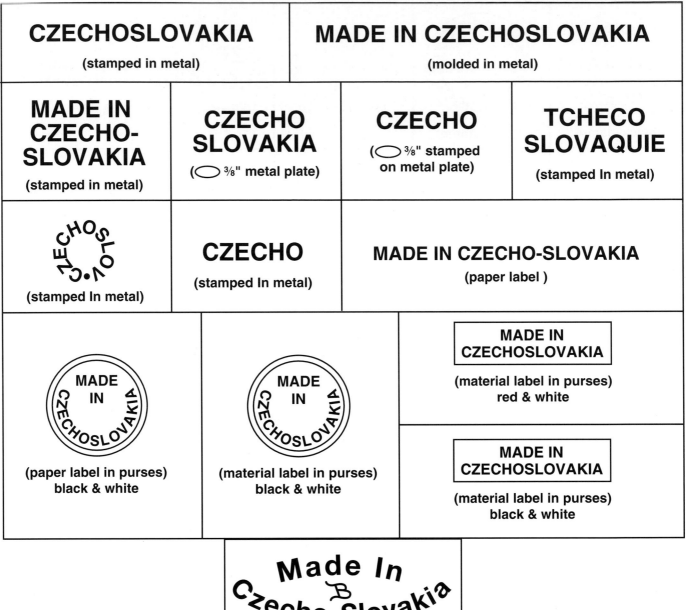

CZECHOSLOVAKIA (stamped in metal)	**MADE IN CZECHOSLOVAKIA** (molded in metal)

MADE IN CZECHO-SLOVAKIA
(stamped in metal)

CZECHO SLOVAKIA
(⬭ ³⁄₈" metal plate)

CZECHO
(⬭ ³⁄₈" stamped on metal plate)

TCHECO SLOVAQUIE
(stamped In metal)

·C·ZECHOSLOV·
(stamped In metal)

CZECHO
(stamped In metal)

MADE IN CZECHO-SLOVAKIA
(paper label)

MADE IN CZECHOSLOVAKIA
(paper label in purses)
black & white

MADE IN CZECHOSLOVAKIA
(material label in purses)
black & white

MADE IN CZECHOSLOVAKIA
(material label in purses)
red & white

MADE IN CZECHOSLOVAKIA
(material label in purses)
black & white

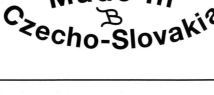

The stickers below are found on most new items from Czechoslovakia.

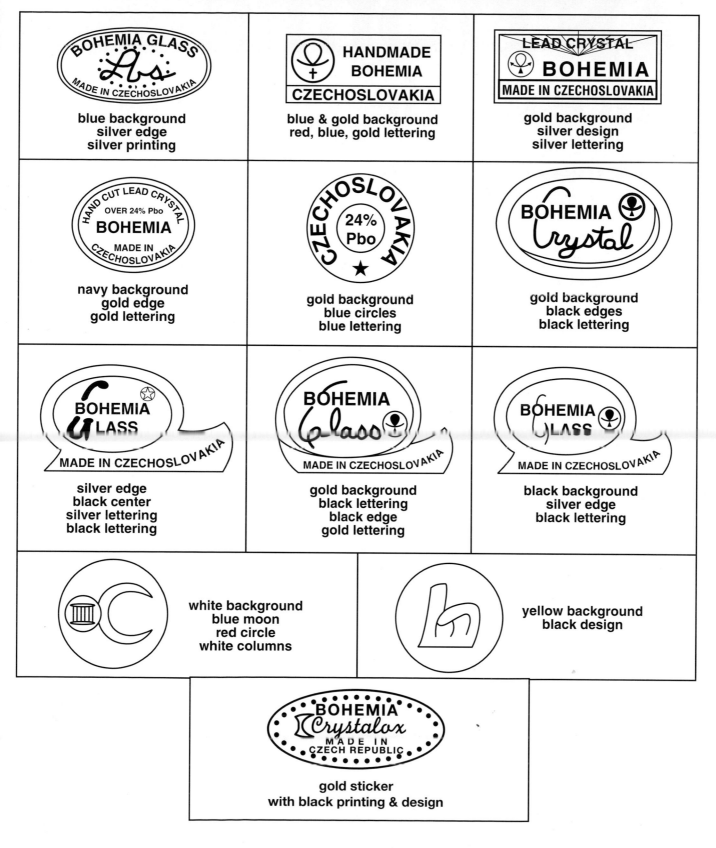

BOHEMIA GLASS — MADE IN CZECHOSLOVAKIA
blue background
silver edge
silver printing

HANDMADE BOHEMIA CZECHOSLOVAKIA
blue & gold background
red, blue, gold lettering

LEAD CRYSTAL BOHEMIA — MADE IN CZECHOSLOVAKIA
gold background
silver design
silver lettering

HAND CUT LEAD CRYSTAL OVER 24% Pbo BOHEMIA MADE IN CZECHOSLOVAKIA
navy background
gold edge
gold lettering

CZECHOSLOVAKIA 24% Pbo
gold background
blue circles
blue lettering

BOHEMIA Crystal
gold background
black edges
black lettering

BOHEMIA GLASS — MADE IN CZECHOSLOVAKIA
silver edge
black center
silver lettering
black lettering

BOHEMIA Glass — MADE IN CZECHOSLOVAKIA
gold background
black lettering
black edge
gold lettering

BOHEMIA GLASS — MADE IN CZECHOSLOVAKIA
black background
silver edge
black lettering

white background
blue moon
red circle
white columns

yellow background
black design

BOHEMIA Crystalox MADE IN CZECH REPUBLIC
gold sticker
with black printing & design